Automation of Trading Machine for Traders

Jacinta Chan

Automation of Trading Machine for Traders

How to Develop Trading Models

palgrave
macmillan

Jacinta Chan
University of Malaya
Kuala Lumpur, Malaysia

ISBN 978-981-13-9944-2 ISBN 978-981-13-9945-9 (eBook)
https://doi.org/10.1007/978-981-13-9945-9

This Palgrave Pivot imprint is published by the registered company Springer Nature Singapore Pte Ltd.
The registered company address is: 152 Beach Road, #21-01/04 Gateway East, Singapore 189721, Singapore

Preface

Opening Position with Trading Almanac (Definitions)

The motivation behind this book is to share the methodology to develop new automated trading models using artificial intelligence approaches to time tested technical indicators for the purpose of trading profitably in today's increasingly difficult and volatile financial markets.

This book begins with the opening position of where we are, what there are in the market and how we can move forward. The opening position starts with the Trading Almanac that holds the genesis of old trading rules and development of new algorithmic trading systems. In this preface, we equip the reader with the range of trading rules that we use.

In this section, the reader is introduced to the tools of the trade. The purpose of laying out the terms and their definitions is to display the basic tools that the new trader will encounter frequently in his or her trading career. He has a choice to decide if the trading tools available in the market are suitable for him. An example would be market analysis that consists of fundamental analysis and technical analysis; it is his choice to choose to use fundamental analysis or technical analysis or a combination of both. At the very least, the reader will know the tools that traders use in general and prepare himself adequately to trade the markets with those who use either discipline.

Knowing the tools will be the first step to learning any trade and so it is with technical analysis, technical indicators, and trading systems.

This section defines the scope of study of technical analysis, technical indicators, trading systems, and trading-related matters, like risk and loss management. The rest of the book concentrates on how you are going to use these basic tools to make yourself an exceptionally successful trader who trades profitably in the long run.

We begin at the base foundation with definitions of the disciplines of market analyses, that traders use. There are at least two conventional market analyses used by market practitioners to explain the behavior of market prices; Technical Analysis and Fundamental Analysis. The academia has a third theory called Random-Walk (Fama, 1965). Other theories supporting technical analysis include fractal geometry (Mandelbrot, 1967; Mandelbrot & Hudson, 2004). To study the patterns, artificial intelligence methods like combinations of artificial neural networks, wavelet denoise transform, and adaptive methods with technical indicators are used (Chan Phooi M'ng & Mehralizadeh, 2016). The most common classical market analyses are fundamental analysis and technical analysis.

Fundamental Analysis, also known as security analysis, is the study of macroeconomic, industry, and company information to derive its intrinsic value, for the purpose of determining if an asset is overvalued or undervalued. A top-down approach would be to analyze current economic conditions, the industry's risks and opportunities, and narrow the analysis down to the company level where the company's past, present, and future potential earnings are analyzed and projected to determine the fair value of the asset. If the market price is lower than the fair value of the asset, the call would be to buy long the asset, or vice versa.

Technical Analysis is the study of price movements using past prices, volume, and open interest to identify trading opportunities. Technical analysis researches the properties of the price series data empirically for patterns or trends to make trading decisions. Technical analysis includes a variety of techniques such as chart analysis for pattern recognition and algorithm technical trading systems for making quantitative trading decision to long or short the security.

The most basic place to start would be to look and observe the price movements in a chart. **Chart** is a graphical record of prices and volume (and open interest in the case of futures contracts), taken at regular intervals, like a day where:

- **Open/Opening price** is the first traded price for the period,
- **High** is the highest price traded for the period,

- **Low** is the lowest price traded for the period, and
- **Close/Closing price** is the last trade price for the period.

Open interest is the number of futures contracts that had been open and are still valid, that had not been closed and **volume** is the number of contracts/shares traded for the period.

With the prices, usually the closing prices, technical indicators are derived. **Technical indicators** are calculated using simple mathematic formula to signal the direction of the price movement. Some of the most popular technical indicators that traders use in general are:

Lagging Indicators like Moving Average (MA): Trading rules that indicate a buy signal when the closing price is above the average price over the previous X number of periods and a sell signal otherwise.

Leading Oscillators like Resistance Strength Index (RSI): Trading rules that calculate when the market is overbought or oversold; indicates a sell signal when the market is overbought and a buy signal when market is oversold.

For traders, the dilemma has always been which indicator to use, as different technical indicators give more accurate signals in different market conditions. Lagging indicators like MA are trend trading indicators and will work very well when market is trending up or down. Leading Indicators like RSI are range trading indicators that work well when markets are trading within certain price ranges. **Trading Range** is a price range in which sideway trading had been confined between Resistance at the top and Support at the bottom for a long period of time. **Resistance** is an area in a chart above the current price where previously prices were not able to penetrate through whereas **Support** is an area at the lower boundary of the trading range where declines halt and reverse. Therefore when market is ranging, Range Trading System should be used. **Range Trading System** is a trading system that tries to sell at the resistance on the assumption that the price increase will halt and the market will pullback, and to buy at the support based on similar market pullback assumption. However, it has been observed and tested empirically that a support does not necessarily imply that prices cannot fall below it. If prices fall through the support, then **Trend Trading Systems** should be applied on the downward break. **Trend Trading System** is trading system with a set of trading rules that define when to initiate a position early to capture the prevailing trend using a mechanically generated signal on the assumption that the **trend** will continue. A **Trend** is the general direction of the prevailing price movement; downtrend is set when prices and resistances are steadily declining, characterized by lower highs and lower lows and uptrend happens when prices and supports are steadily increasing, characterized by higher lows and higher highs. **Algorithm Trading System** is a trading system with a pre-set of trading rules to mathematically compute according to an algorithm that can be used in trending or ranging market, the algorithm adjusting to the prevailing market conditions to mechanically generated signals (long, short, or out-of-market) on when to enter and when to exit, and executes the trades automatically. It involves the use of algorithms that are robust in automated trading. Moving Average is a technical indicators used in trend trading systems. The trading rule would be to long the security when current price is above the moving average and to short the security when current price is below the moving average. **Long** is the act of buying which results in the state of owning a security. **Short** is the state of being short a security which is resulted from the act of selling before buying.

These trading terms trace the history of technical analysis and track its development over the last one and a half century.

One of the first foundations of technical analysis was laid down by Charles Dow (Hamilton, 1922; Nelson, 1903; Rhea, 1932) in a series of Wall Street Journal editorials in the late 1800s. His observations and analysis were later named The **Dow Theory** (Rhea, 1932) which proposes six tenets that became the core foundation of technical analysis. The six basic tenets of Dow Theory are:

- The Averages (Industrial and Transportation) must confirm each other.
- The Averages discount everything.
- The market has three movements.
- The major trends have three phases.
- Volume must confirm trend.
- A trend continues until the signal reverses.

Against technical analysis is random walk theory, a hypothesis that states that the past history of the series cannot be used to predict the future in any meaningful way and that the future path of the price of a security is no more predictable than the path of a series of cumulated random numbers

(Fama, 1965). Fractal Geometry is an observation (Mandelbrot & Hudson, 2004) that states there are repeating patterns in nature and these patterns are found in time series. Artificial intelligence methods like neural network are used in **algorithm trading system** to machine learn these patterns to predict future prices (Chan Phooi M'ng & Mehralizadeh, 2016).

Algorithm Technical Trading System (or Automated or Algo, Black Box or Robo Trading) is the computer program trades execution according to an algorithm that is suitable to the prevailing market conditions. The algorithm in the program is derived after intensive backtesting and optimization. Algorithm trading programs are popularly employed by professional model trading desks of large financial institutions. **Backtest** uses historical data to test for profit using a trading system. **Optimization** is the finding of the best performing parameter for a trading system. **Parameter** is a value used in the trading system to vary and optimize the timing of the signal.

Risk control in the form of **stop-loss order** is also inherent in the automated algorithmic process. The process is automatic, and once implemented, it does not require or allow for subjective trading decision making, human judgment, or interference. The signal generation and stop-loss level are the results of the algorithms that the quantitative analyst programs in.

Before professional traders trade, they have **trading plans**. These plans are their trading edge that charts the future of their trading experience to be that of net positive return. Therefore, their trading plans are usually based on historical patterns of statistical price returns. They plan their trading before they begin and they begin with research.

Strange as it may be, many people who are trading in stocks, futures, and foreign exchange do not know what they are doing. They repeatedly lose money for the same common reason and they do not even know why. The most common reason is they fail to cut loss early and even after the loss has been cut, they cannot accept or contemplate why they had to lose at all. This book attempts to lay out some of the pitfalls, so that you can avoid the same common mistakes made by amateur traders. It is the objective of this book that you can make it to become a professional trader and trade successfully, profitably.

This book is arranged to cover the above areas in a systematic manner for the apprentice to learn, understand, and apply the different tools to need to make it as a professional trader. Anyone can be a trader but only those who have undergone and passed professional technical training and are trading seriously can be a professional trader. The areas that are important in the science of trading begin with the foundation of the technical analysis which is the cornerstone of professional trading. The areas which are important in basic technical analysis are: learning to chart, classical reversal and continuation patterns, trends, moving averages, momentum, range breakouts, projection levels, explaining risk and returns and finally what we are looking to design and develop, the trading system.

The objectives of this book are:

- Learn how to construct, read and interpret your own chart.
- Construct common technical indicators like moving average and momentum and put them to use for your trading.
- Identify the profit-making opportunities and the possible projections of how far the trend will carry.
- Learn the basics of a trading system.

This book will introduce the concepts involved in algorithm trading.

The basic concepts discussed here are:

- trading algorithms;
- optimized parameters;
- robustness;
- high return to low risk;
- average gain must far exceed average loss;
- no unexpected losses;
- ability to avoid whipsaws;
- ability to enter new trends early;
- ability to automatically adjust;
- efficient execution.

In pivot book, we study in depth the first steps to becoming a professional trader, including:

1. Drawing your own trading plan and selecting what technical indicators to use;
2. Conducting your own data research;
3. Designing your own professional algorithm trading system;

4. Writing out your trading system using mathematical formulas;
5. Programming your own mechanical trading system;
6. Knowing the necessary capital requirements;
7. Managing risk and losses;
8. Conducting your own trade evaluation.

To trade in any market, the most basic tool necessary is the chart of its historical prices. It is important to see where the prices have been and where it is now and where they are likely to be headed. Therefore, the study of prices and their behaviors are essential for any investor who wants to profitably trade any commodity in the long run. Care has been taken to ensure that data and information areaccurate and correct; neither the author nor the publisher accepts responsibility for any loss occasioned to any person who either acts or refrains from acting as a result of any statement in this book. The author is not recommending the purchase or sale of any particular financial security as references to any financial security are made for illustration only.

Kuala Lumpur, Malaysia Jacinta Chan

References

Chan Phooi M'ng, J., & Mehralizadeh, M. (2016). Forecasting East Asian Indices futures via a novel hybrid of wavelet-PCA denoising and artificial neural network models. *PLOS One, 11*(6), e0156338.

Fama, E. (1965). Random walks in stock market prices. *Financial Analyst Journal, 16,* 1–16.

Graham, B., & Dodd, D. (1934). *Security analysis* (1st ed.). New York: Whittlesey House.

Hamilton, W. (1922). *The stock market barometer.* New York: Nabu Press.

Mandelbrot, B. (1967). The variation of the prices of cotton, wheat and railroad stocks and of some financial rates. *The Journal of Business, 40,* 393–413.

Mandelbrot, B., & Hudson, R. (2004). *The (mis)behaviour of markets: A fractal view of risk, ruin and reward.* London: Profile Books Ltd.

Nelson, S. (1903). *The ABC of stock speculation.* New York: S.A. Nelson.

Rhea, R. (1932). *The Dow theory.* New York: Fraser Publishing Co.

Acknowledgements

God makes all things possible, including this book. This book is the result of the contributions of many people whom God brings together.

This book did not happen overnight. It took the efforts of many individuals from different backgrounds and parts of the world whom I have come to know as friends over the years. I thank my editors, Ruth Noble, Sophia Siegler and Shukkanthy Siva, from Palgrave Macmillan for their guidance and efficient work. I thank all my friends, my colleagues, Professor Dr. Azlinna, Professor Dr. Ibrahim Mohamed, Professor Dr. Mohd Nazari Ismail and Universiti Malaya, research grant team members, Dr. Azmin, Dr. Fadiya, Kevin Ngui, Foong Cheng Ho, Ham Yi Jer and associates, Dr. Xie Yinhao, my beloved students, Dr. Ali Mehr, (I thank MBA graduates, Kelvin Chong Kok Kean, Kevin, Cheng Ho, and Shirley Lau for winning one of the top prizes in 2018 CME Trading Challenge) and readers whose support make all my books bestsellers. I thank all my family, James, Hayley, especially my lovely mother, Veronica Yap Chin Tuck and my late father, Michael Chan Kok Heong for their constant and everlasting love and support. Most importantly, I thank God, my Lord Jesus Christ, for all these wonderful family, friends, colleagues, students, editors and the great teachers, academicians like Professor Dr. Eugene Fama, Professor Dr. Eugene Stanley, Professor Dr. Morton Lane, Professor Dr. Ramazan Gençay, Professor Dr. Alejandro Raul Hernandez Montoya, Professor Dr. Boris Podobnik,

Professor Dr. Mark Taylor, and fellow market technicians like Larry Williams whom I have come to know as friends who contribute to the success of this book.

Thank you.

Jacinta Chan

Contents

List of Figures

List of Tables

CHAPTER 1

Introduction to Model Trading

Abstract Financial markets' volatility appeals to investors because of their high attractive returns and to academicians who are obsessed with pattern modeling to predict the future. The objective of this chapter is to provide a background of fundamental analysis and technical analysis; the tools market practitioners use. This chapter begins with trading rules and how these trading rules find and develop their way in the science of technical analysis and modern finance. It traces to the need for more advanced technical analysis tools and the introduction of automated algorithm trading systems. Algorithm trading is preferred in today's proprietary trading desks because it has been rigorously tested and proven to have a statistical edge that generates net positive return above passive benchmark buy-and-hold. This book discusses how to develop trading systems that suit different market conditions.

Keywords Technical analysis · Fundamental analysis · Algorithm trading · Professional model trading · Automated trading system

People are interested in these financial instruments mainly because they are motivated to find the high returns of these instruments. Financial markets possess a fluctuating and volatile nature, which makes them appealing to a variety of people for different reasons, including investors who are attracted to them because of high returns and researchers who are eager to model market trends as a disciplined science to decipher future patterns.

J. Chan, *Automation of Trading Machine for Traders*,
https://doi.org/10.1007/978-981-13-9945-9_1

These high returns over short periods of time are due to high volatilities in these particular markets. Today's market technicians usually use technical analysis and related scientific tools to trade in the financial markets they specialize in. They use price charts and formulas to make trading decisions. Some market technicians use purely algorithms to make these objective decisions to enter and exit markets; this book concentrates on these algorithm technical indicators they design, test, and apply to the markets of their choice, for profit maximization. Algorithm trading models have evolved exponentially in recent years due to more rapid reactions to temporary mispricing and easier price management with computational trading systems, which can learn from thousands of information sources without the hindrance of human emotions. Thus, technical analysis, the methodology and science of deciphering past historical data to forecast future prices, has also grown to include machine learning methods, like the artificial neural network (ANN) approach.

The objective of this chapter is to provide a background of market analysis, which comprises fundamental and technical analyses which are the tools that market practitioners are using. It begins with the old trading rules and how they find and develop their way in technical analysis and modern finance. It traces the development of the need for more advanced technical analysis tool that may be of more value to today's evolution of algorithm trading and the introduction of automated algorithm trading systems. The construction of a trading system begins with the age-old mechanical trading rules. The apprentice trader is guided to understand the beginning of constructing basic trading system.

Technical analysis is the study of historical prices. It observes the past behaviors to understand its current trend, which may give an indication of its immediate future direction (Murphy, 1999). Besides professional technical analysts, chartists, and fund managers, anyone who has an interest in the price movements will profit from the knowledge of technical analysis. Technical analysis is not an art for the few talented, gifted individuals as some chartists will lead the mass public to believe. It is a well-structured and organized science; that is, the same results can be replicated from the formulas and technical indicators by anyone. The foundation of technical analysis is built on the tenets observed by Charles Dow (Rhea, 1932).

To understand the basic and basis of technical analysis, it is important to start right at the base, at the foundation tenets. This chapter covers the introduction of using technical analysis approach to trading. To begin, this section defines the market technician who trades using Dow Theory and technical analysis.

Market Analysis

There are at least two conventional disciplines used by market practitioners to explain the behavior of market prices: technical analysis and fundamental analysis. The academia has a third theory called "Random-Walk" (Fama, 1965). Other methods that are gaining popularity are combinations of ANNs (Chan Phooi M'ng & Mehralizadeh, 2016), genetic programming, and adaptive methods with technical indicators (Chan Phooi M'ng, 2018).

Technical Analysis

Technical analysis researches the properties of the price series data empirically for patterns or trends to make trading decisions (Edwards & Magee, 2008). Technical analysis includes a variety of techniques such as chart analysis, pattern recognition, seasonality and cycle analysis, and algorithm technical trading systems.

One of the first foundations of technical analysis was laid down by Charles Dow in a series of *Wall Street Journal* editorials in the late 1800s. Although Dow, the editor of *Wall Street Journal*, wrote both technical analysis as well as fundamental reports on the market, his followers held onto his technical analysis of markets and named his observations Dow Theory (Rhea, 1932).

The views held by professional analysts, both technical analysts and the fundamental analysts, believe that certain trends exist in the market while the views held by traditional academicians subscribe to the theory that the randomness in historical prices series cannot be used to predict future prices in any meaningful way.

Traditionally, there are at least two major schools of thought regarding trends and the potential ability to profit from them, Dow Theory (technical analysis) and fundamental analysis. If there was a third school, it would be one that was attended by traditional academicians who advocated random walk theory. Mainstream academic research regards stock prices as random time sequences that contain noise (Fama, 1965). In contrast, market practitioners and proponents of technical analysis believe that past patterns and trends will be repeated in the future, and the skill and knowledge to identify these trends can be gainfully used to generate abnormal returns (Andrada-Felix & Fernandez-Rodriguez, 2008). Technical analysis establishes specific trading rules using specific indicators such as moving average to decipher behavioral patterns out of time-series data (Gencay & Stengos, 1998). Gencay and Stengos (1998) find that the key advantage behind the moving average rule is that it provides a means of determining the general direction or trend of a market based on historical behavior of stock prices. The added advantage of the moving average rule is the ability to capture information in nonlinear time-series prices that are usually ignored by methods that assume linearity.

As technical analysis develops into more rigorous, quantitative, and scientifically based research methods, new theories emerge. Computational algorithm trading systems may be the preferred trading systems of the day as they are used by the practicing professional market technicians in large institutions. Combination methods using technical rules and adaptive methods, genetic programming, and ANNs to find and create superior trading rules that generate net positive abnormal returns seem to be the latest trend in time series.

This section elaborates on these main ideas. First, the development of technical analysis begins with Dow Theory. Second, the basic tenets, principles, and concepts of technical analysis are explained. Third, technical analysis is compared with fundamental analysis. Fourth, these two investment methods are compared with random walk theory that deems technical analysis and fundamental analysis to be of no value since price series follow unpredictable random walks (Fama, 1965). Finally, with computer generations, combinations of technical rules involving genetic programming, ANN, and adaptive methods dominate the most current academic studies (Andrada-Felix & Fernandex-Rodriguez, 2008).

The first organized school of thought on movements of price series is Dow Theory (Rhea, 1932). Dow Theory is based on the observations and analysis of the US stock market by Charles Dow in a series of Review and Outlook editorials in *The Wall Street Journal* from the late nineteenth century to 1902. Charles Dow was the editor and founder of *The Wall Street Journal* and the creator of Dow Jones Industrial Average. Charles Dow, the part owner of *Wall Street Journal*, penned down his observations and analysis of the US stock market in a series of Review and Outlook editorials in the *Wall Street Journal.* His observations and analysis were later named the Dow Theory (Rhea, 1932) which proposes six tenets that became the core foundation of technical analysis.

The six basic tenets of Dow Theory are:

1. The averages (industrial and transportation) must confirm each other.
2. The averages discount everything.
3. The market has three movements.
4. The major trends have three phases.
5. Volume must confirm trend.
6. A trend continues until the signal reverses.

These six tenets have been observed and used over a century of stock trading by many market practitioners of technical analysis. These tenets are further developed into what they called Dow Theory by Nelson (1903), Hamilton (1922), and Rhea (1932) who concentrate on the price movements of the averages (mainly industrial and transportation). These six tenets are the basic foundation on which technical analysis is built.

The market's three movements are:

1. Primary movements (lasting for years);
2. Secondary correction movements (lasting for months); and
3. Daily fluctuations.

In a bull primary movement, the three phases are:

1. Accumulation;
2. Big up move (uptrend); and
3. Excess.

In a bear primary movement, the three phases are:

1. Distribution;
2. Big down move (Downtrend); and
3. Despair.

The phases of the primary movements are depicted in Fig. 1.1.

Technical analysis is the study of historical data, which includes prices and volume, to identify trends for trading and investment purposes. As an approach to market analysis, technical analysis is based on the general principle that historical prices tend to repeat themselves in regular patterns.

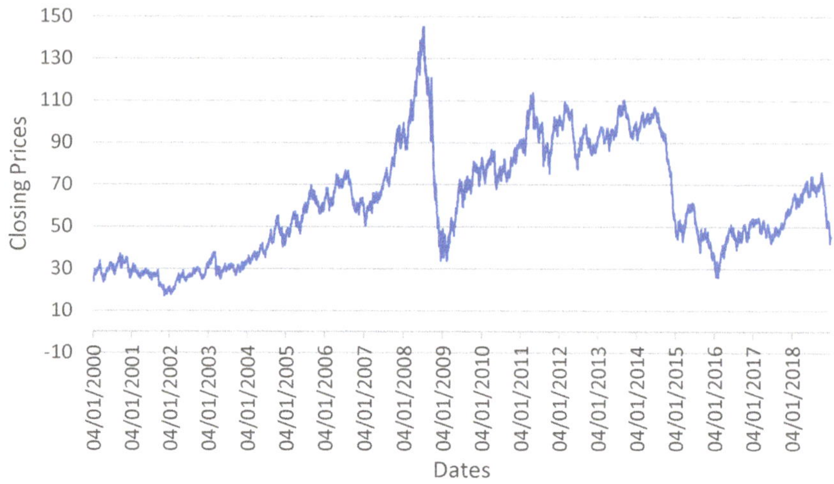

Fig. 1.1 Chart of CLOF depicting Accumulation, uptrend, excess, distribution, downtrend, and despair (*Source* Author's creation of chart of CLOF depicting accumulation, uptrend, excess, distribution, downtrend, and despair based on CLOF closing prices)

Basically, the general principles underlying technical analysis are:

- All information is incorporated in the price.
- Prices tend to move in trends.
- Price patterns tend to repeat.

These imply that the recurring price patterns can provide signs to probable future price movements and trends. Thus, the way to trade equity and commodity futures is to identify patterns or signals that indicate the beginnings of new trends. Technical analysis states that the financial markets move in trends and these trends can be identified to generate appropriate buy or sell signal to trade profitably. The underlying belief, therefore, is that there are systematic statistical dependences in asset returns.

Traders employ two general types of technical analysis: charting and mechanical trading rules. Charting involves qualitative techniques of price patterns observation and recognition in graphs from the past price history to predict future price movements. Charting relies on subjective judgment and skill in price patterns recognition. Mechanical technical trading rules involve quantitative techniques that rely on algorithm technical indicators. These technical indicators are based on objective mathematical functions of present and past prices. With technical indicators, trading performance can be measured, and this is a very good form of discipline for the market technician.

Technical indicators can be categorized into two groups: lagging indicators and leading indicators. Lagging indicators, like moving averages, are usually trend-following indicators that perform well in a trending market. Trend-following indicators work on the assumption that the prevailing trend is likely to continue. However, if the market is not trending, lagging trend-following indicators tend to give many false signals. Entries into the market on these false signals result in whipsaws. Whipsaws are a series of continuous small losses that reflect negatively in the equity performance.

Leading indicators are usually indicators that perform well in a ranging market as they anticipate reversals and the next price movements. If the market ranges between the previous support and resistance, leading indicators tend to perform well but not otherwise. However, if the market is trending, leading indicators will result in huge losses which is detrimental to capital preservation.

Therefore, one of the limitations of technical analysis tools is their ability of providing correct trading signals in a specific market condition only. Because of this limitation, it is difficult for the market technician to decide which indicators, like moving average, moving average crossover, or moving average envelope to use.

This book focuses on lagging technical indicators, moving average, because they are trending indicators that try to capture the large profits that can be found in heavy tails of the price changes distributions.

Market technicians today use programs to chart prices and technical indicators to make trading decisions. To maximize profits from the market, they are constantly searching for the trading systems that produce the most positive abnormal returns. Systematic backtesting is applied to technical indicators to select the most optimal trading system that produces the most net profit consistently at minimal risk. We systematically design, develop, and test AMA′ and compare it with other known technical indicators like moving averages. The systematic backtesting of AMA′ is solely concerned with using only past historical price series to identify probable future trend using technical analysis indicators like moving averages.

Some market practitioners might look to explain technical analysis using behavior finance, while some others, like Mandelbrot and Hudson (2004), founder of fractal geometry, see repeating patterns in time series which he states is the basis for technical analysis. Others may prefer to explain price in terms of value, and this value investing is popularly known as fundamental analysis (Grahams & Dobb, 1934).

Fundamental Analysis

The second organized school of thought picked up Dow's earlier studies on the value investing and developed these concepts into a formal study of security analysis, commonly known by market practitioners as fundamental analysis. Led by academicians like Professors Benjamin Graham and David Dodd (1934) who authored the book, Security Analysis, this second school of organized thought is built up into an important study and research of stocks and stock markets, under the discipline of finance taught by universities worldwide.

This finance discipline is called fundamental analysis by brokers and traders and generally is a prerequisite knowledge for entering into the profession of research in financial and capital markets, trading, and dealing. Fundamental analysis is formally defined as the study of economic information to estimate intrinsic values and to gauge if an asset is overvalued or undervalued. Fundamental analysis looks in depth at the financial conditions and operating results of a specific company and the underlying behavior of its common stock. The value of a stock is established by analyzing the fundamental information associated with the company such as accounting profit, competition, and management.

Generally, fundamental analysis evaluates the economic condition of the country it operates in as well the international economy, the industry and the factors affecting the industry and finally the company itself to determine the intrinsic value of the share. If the intrinsic value is higher than the market price, a buy recommendation will be issued by the research analyst. Similarly, if the intrinsic value is lower than the market price, the recommendation would be a sell.

With modeling growing in significance in the finance industry, all information and data considered relevant to the price of the stock are being quantified into mathematical models by the quantitative analyst. The subjective traditional decision-making method using fundamental analysis by the fund manager is fast being replaced by proprietary algorithm models that incorporate all relevant fundamental data the quantitative analyst considers important. Even so, the selection of relevant data that the quantitative analyst considers important is subjective.

However, it can be argued that most stocks cannot be accurately valued due to the inadequate and misrepresentation of the facts and values attached to the management and the future of the company, the industry, and the economy at large. The fundamental factors are overshadowed by the supply and demand of the stock. The market price reflects the current supply and demand of the stock. Therefore, the market price is different from the perceived value of the stock.

Part of the reason why a security analyst has enormous difficulty in forecasting the future of a company prospects and market price is because of the influence of random events. Fama (1965) initiated another school of thought that states in a Random-Walk Market, on the average, a security chosen by a mediocre fundamental analyst will produce a return no better than a return from a randomly selected security of the same general riskiness. Fama (1965) and his academic colleagues believe that no investor can achieve excess return above the benchmark return from the buy-and-hold policy based on the historical and present information. Random walk theory implies that the past history of the series cannot be used to predict the future in any meaningful way and that the future path of the price of a security is no more predictable than the path of a series of cumulated random numbers (Fama, 1965).

On the other hand, Mandelbrot (1967) states that although the prices may seem random, there are patterns that can be calculated using power-law scaling as in fractal geometry. Fractal geometry is a branch of mathematics that concerns with seemingly irregular patterns made up of fractal parts that are in some way similar as a whole. It is a method of measuring Chaos theory with geometric shapes. Using scaling or power law, Mandelbrot and Hudson (2004) calculates an alpha for the price changes of a commodity. Stanley, Plerou, and Xavier (2008) and Podobnik and Stanley (2008) find evidence for scaling and cross correlations in financial times series.

Algorithm Technical Trading Systems

Algorithm trading has evolved in recent years due to easier price discovery and automated arbitraging to temporary mispricing with computational trading systems, which can learn from multiple information sources without the hindrance of human emotions. Technical analysis has thus grown to include machine learning methods, like the ANN approach.

Accompanying this interest, there has been a number of studies of computational trading algorithms that users find useful for investment timing (Gencay & Stengos, 1998; Lo, Mamaysky, & Wang, 2000; Lukac, Brorsen, & Irwin, 1990).

The problem confronting most financial market traders is how to differentiate a ranging market (when the price movements are confined between a lower boundary of support and an upper boundary of resistance) from a trending market (when prices are steadily moving in a general upward or downward direction). It is important for the trader to correctly identify the market condition, as a ranging market requires technical analysis tools (such as leading momentum rate of change) that differ from those employed in a trending market (like lagging moving average). Identifying the wrong market condition and employing the wrong trading strategy can result in unnecessary losses known as whipsaws.

An algorithm trading system is the most important component of the professional model trading desk of any financial institution that conducts proprietary trading. It accounts for the disciplined trading of a responsible professional trader and financial institution. This is opposed to the collapse of a financial institution due to rogue trading. These trading algorithms have been researched and tested to have a statistical edge. Inherent in trading systems are risk control mechanisms. All signals are automated.

The algorithm trading system is constructed using a simple set of mechanical trading rules selected after a series of tests to generate the most profitable trading signals at acceptable accumulative consecutive small losses.

The trading rules consist of algorithms with optimized parameters to indicate trading signals. The trading signal is either to long or to short an asset or a contract. Most of these models are developed by a trader for his or her own trading use, and it is highly unlikely that they will be shared with the public.

The reason why trading algorithms are preferred in today's proprietary trading desks is that the resulting systems have been rigorously tested and proven to have a statistical edge that generates net positive returns above the passive benchmark buy-and-hold policy.

The quantitative analyst or algorithm quant trader designs, tests, and develops the algorithms that automate all trading decisions and executions. The algorithms developed are selected to be the best performers before they are validated and implemented. The algorithms are selected, innovated, and intensively tested to suit the markets that these quantitative traders are trading in. Extensive research is conducted to select the algorithms, usually innovated from existing technical indicators like moving average (Brock, Lakonishok, & LeBaron, 1992; Lukac, Brorsen, & Irwin, 1988) and standard deviation.

Backtests and live tests are conducted repeatedly using different contracts and timeframes. The parameters for the technical indicators are optimized to suit past, and hopefully future, prices. The parameters are optimized using trading programs that give maximum profit and the least amount of consecutive losses, using the most recent historical data. This exercise is conducted periodically to enable a better fit to the current data Different parameters are used for different markets and timeframes. The parameters generally correlate with the volatility of the markets. In a higher volatility and faster market, a shorter period parameter is used, and vice versa. In a shorter timeframe, such as hourly, a shorter period parameter is used and vice versa.

Algorithm trading is preferred to traditional discretionary trading because not only are all trading decisions objective and quantifiable when audited, but the algorithms are tested to provide a statistical edge: that is, the expectation of positive returns based on backtesting of returns of past data. The backtests must show a net profit after taking into consideration transaction costs and losses.

Algorithms for automated trading are sets of trading rules or combinations of trading rules. These algorithms are often designed to generate automated signals from basic statistical concepts, time-series analysis, quantitative methods, and probabilities. If the automated trading system's probability of winning trades is equal to that of losing trades, and the average gain far exceeds the average loss (after taking into consideration transaction costs), the net result of this automated trading can only be net profit.

The hardest things for trend trading systems to avoid are whipsaws in a range market. Frequent small losses that accumulate in a range market usually wipe away gains from large trend movements. Therefore, the best that trending systems can do in range trading is to do nothing: do no trade or hold on to one side of the position (either long or short) until the trend sets in.

The quant trader has to find an algorithm (formula) that defines when the market is range trading and when it is trend trading. When a trend sets in, it is important to get into it early to enjoy the maximum profit rather than waiting for a longer confirmation, by which time short trends in volatile markets would have ended. It is imperative that the quant trader must find the appropriate algorithm that defines when range trading ends and trend trading begins. The quant trader must not only find an appropriate algorithm that distinguishes between range trading and trend trading but must also innovate the algorithm to automatically adjust its parameters to suit the two different market conditions. The trading system must be able to adjust its parameters automatically to be longer term in a range market to avoid whipsaws and to be short term in a trend market to enter into new trends early.

This book will discuss how to develop a trading system to suit different trading conditions. This book guides beginner trader through the process of charting, reading charts with technical indicators and writing trading plans according to projected returns against expected risks. If used with discipline, it is the short cut to become a professional trader because the tools and techniques are all clearly spelt out distinctly in different chapters.

Setup of a Model Trading Desk

The objective of the model trading desk would be to achieve net profit higher than the benchmark return from the buy-and-hold policy or the risk-free interest rate and to limit its maximum drawdown to no more than a fraction of its highest profit, while managing its risk.

To set up our trading operations, we first learn the functions of a professional model trading desk. This consists of a head of proprietary trading who may also be the designer of the algorithm trading systems and/or who assesses and approves the algorithm trading systems that his or her traders design for different markets. The trader who designs the algorithm trading system is responsible for it, and his income is closely tied to its trading performance. This algorithm trading system must first be validated by the quantitative model validator and approved by the head of proprietary trading who has the authority to set a certain level of acceptable possible loss predicted by the trading system based on past performance.

A proprietary model trading desk's checklist would consist of the following:

- proprietary trading algorithms systems;
- data analysis and research;
- track record, backtesting, and optimization;
- many different markets and trading instruments;
- different trading techniques;
- trading rules;
- live monitoring of positions and risk management;
- capital allocation and management to capture trends and profits;
- periodic evaluation and fine–tuning; and
- efficient, unemotional, and mechanical execution.

The audit, compliance, and risk management departments ensure that the trader executes the trade according to the algorithm trading system that has been approved and the position is accompanied by a trailing stop loss which is decided on entry of the position within the limit of approved loss. The back office clears the trade and ensures an appropriate margin is maintained for the position with the exchange's clearinghouse.

The position is maintained and the loss (or profit) is monitored live by the risk management department until the position is closed by an offsetting trade. If there is a loss from marked-to-market activity at the end of each trading day, the back office will remit the necessary margin top-up to the clearinghouse the following day before trading begins. In an integrated system, while the finance department will be immediately alerted to this outflow of funds, the management's urgent attention will also be captured if there is any anomaly.

Writing the rules and building the system may seem like a lot of research and hard work but it is, in fact, the simple part. The harder part is the disciplined act of following the chosen trading system exactly. This is depicted by the dealing desk where dealers execute the orders they receive from traders mechanically and without emotion. Their performance bonuses, if any, will be based on making minimal or no execution mistakes and slippage.

For the trading house, the two functions of trading and dealing are rightly separated and therefore no emotions or egos are involved. For the trader, these two functions are performed by an individual who must therefore follow the trading system exactly, without any emotion or ego.

While this book will help you design and build your trading system, I must stress to the apprentice trader that you must follow your chosen system at all times. This is because the trading system that you have chosen, from among many, has been researched and backtested many times and will probably have a proven track record.

In fact, the head of a proprietary desk will be looking at potential new traders' track records when they come for interviews for trading positions. The head of model trading will note whether the house is prepared to withstand the maximum consecutive losses that a model can potentially give. Real-time, online monitoring of these positions and the risks they represent is absolutely essential. One risk officer might be assigned to be solely responsible for monitoring the positions of the entire house. However, each trader should be responsible for monitoring the stop loss (maximum loss per trade) of his or her own position. Of course, the head of model trading, or the trader him or herself, can readjust the parameters to improve trading performance on a regular basis.

The trading technique here is to have a wide range of investments to choose from to ensure the highest return to risk ratio, to define trend trading from range trading (for it is trend trading that offers the higher return), and to have enough markets to trade as markets do not trend all the time.

All trades must then be executed using the approved automated trading system. Besides transaction costs, slippage of at least two ticks must be given, one for entry and another for exit.

Individual trade risks are managed at the trade level, which means that stop loss must be placed at the point of entry of each position. While each individual trader is responsible for his own position/loss monitoring, a risk and compliance officer for the entire desk is responsible to monitor that the entire risk portfolio, the instrument risk portfolio, and the individual market risk portfolio, shall not exceed the permissible risk, the level of which can be an amount or ratio given to him by higher management. He must also monitor that each trader shall not exceed his daily permissible risk and that the accumulated losses of each trader are within his loss limit, the amount of which had been specified to him.

The automated trading system must, therefore, meet the following criteria:

1. Ability to be robust in different markets, in different timeframes;
2. Risk to return ratio of less than one to three;
3. Number of winning trades to losing trades of more than 50%;
4. Capital preservation, low maximum drawdown with inherent loss control mechanism;
5. Ability to avoid some of the whipsaws in range trading market, ability to enter a new trend early and ability to automatically adjust or fine-tune to trend versus range market conditions.

Conclusion: Risk of Not Having an Algorithm Trading System

The proprietary house business is separated from the agency business. There are no emotions or egos involved in professional trading (traders get taps on their shoulders and lose their jobs if they do not perform). Traders are prepared to lose a little in order to win a lot.

The apparent benefit of using a systematic technique which is incorporated into a well-defined algorithm trading system are:

- All signals generated are mechanical. When the trading decisions have been mechanized, the interfering emotions of greed and fear which consume so many uninformed traders are removed.
- The trader can concentrate on improving his particular algorithm trading system and execute his trades accordingly. Consistent execution according to a proven trading system that has been backtested will eventually ensure potential profitability.
- Inherent in this mechanical trading system is an inbuilt risk control mechanism called stop loss. By consistently practicing this stop-loss early program and by letting profits run their course, the net performance result of a disciplined trader can be net profit.

The main consequences of not having and following a tested algorithm trading system are:

1. The risk of ruin, that is, losses can be so huge and uncontrollable that it can ruin a financial institution;
2. There are no stop-loss mechanism and stop-loss level decided upon at the point of entry; and
3. There is no mechanism, device, or procedure to cross-check, monitor the losses, and stop them early when necessary.

Without an a priori algorithm, if a position had been cut by anyone other than the trader himself, there will be cause for contention and argument, should the market turn back in favor of the original position.

With a known algorithm that includes a stop-loss order, any loss is defined and expected at the point of entry. Stop-loss order at the point of entry is therefore a good risk management measure to define and control loss. When the market moves against the position, the loss is automatically stopped out early without any reference to human judgment and emotions. Therefore, an algorithm trading system with well-defined stop loss and limit is an important component of professional model trading.

The conclusion drawn here is that the most severe consequence of not having and using an algorithm trading system is the ruin of the financial institution that has a proprietary trading desk but no well-defined trading system.

This book shows how to develop simple algorithm trading system, like adjustable moving average prime (AMA′), to recognize and trade according to changes in market conditions as soon as possible, to significantly improve the profit performance of a quant desk.

Review: The First Trading Lesson

The first lesson as a trader is to have a strong background in quantitative finance and data analysis to build an adaptive robust algorithm trading system. This is the statistical trading tool that all professional traders have.

- The algorithm trading system must be robust in any market and any timeframe.
- It must have a high return to low risk (loss) ratio with a low maximum drawdown as well as an inherent loss control mechanism.
- The numbers of winning trades must be more than the losing trades and the average gain higher than the average loss.
- The amount of capital must be enough to withstanding the maximum drawdown.
- The algorithm trading system must be able to avoid most whipsaws and yet be able to enter into new emerging trends early.
- The most important robustness test is that the algorithm trading system is able to adapt or fine-tune to adjust to different market condition, range, or trend.

Old trading systems like moving averages system that used to work well in the past do not work as well as they used to in mature markets (Olson, 2004) because other traders know where the buying and selling levels are. To survive in this competitive industry, the trader has to differentiate himself from the crowd by having a more robust and sensitive trading system that is able to detect trend more accurately and enter the market at earliest opportunity possible. So, as the markets mature, we have to find new innovative trading systems to find excess profit.

With the completion of this chapter, the trader now possess the essential technical analysis knowledge to proceed. The next part of this book is the exciting bit about being your own trader but you have to do your own research on the technical indicators to use to start building your own trading system.

Last word on this topic:
Trading with a Trading System

- One of the first decisions that the trader must make, is what trading tools that he is going to use to build his robust profitable trading system. This decision and the trading system have to be well researched to have statistical winning edge on the assets traded.
- All trading decisions must be made on a selected trading system that has been well researched and backtested as profitable in the past, in the carefully selected trading instruments.
- All buy or sell signals must be mechanical and based on certain formulas that can be programmed into a trading system.
- In this well defined trading system, the most important element incorporated is risk management or loss control. Losses control is the key to capital preservation.
- In professional trading, evaluation and fine-tuning need to be done periodically.

The learning objectives of this part are to guide you step-by-step through the phases of:

- research and data analysis,
- designing, and programming your own trading system,
- writing your own trading plan,
- trading professionally with risk and loss management, and adequate capital requirements.

We will use very simple, basic statistics, and run backtest and optimization tests using quantitative methods.

References

Andrada-Felix, J., & Fernandex-Rodriguez, F. (2008). Improving moving average trading rules with boosting and statistical learning methods. *Journal of Forecasting, 27*(5), 433–449.

Brock, W., Lakonishok, J., & LeBaron, B. (1992, December). Simple technical trading rules and the stochastic properties of stock returns. *Journal of Finance, 47*(5), 1731–1764.

Chan Phooi M'ng, J. (2018). Dynamically adjustable moving average (AMA′) technical analysis indicator to forecast Asian Tigers' futures markets. *Physica A: Statistical Mechanics and Its Applications, 509*, 336–345.

Chan Phooi M'ng, J., & Mehralizadeh, M. (2016). Forecasting East Asian indices futures via a novel hybrid of wavelet-PCA denoising and artificial neural network models. *PLOS One, 11*(6), e0156338.

Edwards, R. D., & Magee, J. (2008). *Technical analysis of stock trends* (9th ed.). Chicago, IL: John Magee Inc.

Fama, E. (1965). Random walks in stock market prices. *Financial Analyst Journal, 16*, 1–16.

Gencay, R., & Stengos, T. (1998). Moving average rules, volume and the predictability of security returns with feedforward networks. *Journal of Forecasting, 17*(5–6), 401–414.

Graham, B., & Dodd, D. (1934). *Security analysis* (1st ed.). New York: Whittlesey House.

Hamilton, W. (1922). *The stock market barometer*. New York: Nabu Press.

Lee, C., Gleason, K., & Mathur, I. (2001). Trading rule profits in Latin American currency spot rates. *International Review of Financial Analysis, 10*(2), 135–159.

Lo, A., Mamaysky, H., & Wang, J. (2000). Foundations of technical analysis: Computational algorithms, statistical inference and empirical implementation. *Journal of Finance, 55*(4), 1705–1765.

Lukac, L., Brorsen, B., & Irwin, S. (1988). Similarity of computer guided technical trading systems. *Journal of Futures Markets, 8*(1–13), 64.

Lukac, L., Brorsen, B., & Irwin, S. (1990). *A comparison of twelve technical trading systems*. Greenville, SC: Traders Press Inc.

Mandelbrot, B. (1967). The variation of the prices of cotton, wheat and railroad stocks and of some financial rates. *The Journal of Business, 40*, 393–413.

Mandelbrot, B., & Hudson, R. (2004). *The (mis)behaviour of markets: A fractal view of risk, ruin and reward*. London: Profile Books Ltd.

Murphy, J. (1999). *Technical analysis of the financial markets*. New York: Wiley.

Nelson, S. (1903). *The ABC of stock speculation*. New York: S.A. Nelson.

Olson, D. (2004). Have trading rule profits in the currency markets declined over time? *Journal of Banking & Finance, 28*, 85–105.

Podobnik, B., & Stanley, H. (2008). Detrended cross-correlation analysis: A new method for analysing two nonstationary time series. *Physical Review Letters, 100*(8), 084102.

Rhea, R. (1932). *The Dow theory*. New York: Fraser Publishing Co.

Stanley, E., Plerou, X., & Xavier, G. (2008). A statistical physics view of financial fluctuations: Evidence for scaling and universality. *Physica A: Statistical Mechanics and its Applications, 387*(15), 3967–3981.

CHAPTER 2

Technical Indicators: Market Technicians Trading Tools

Abstract Technical indicators are tools of the trade that market technicians use to determine the trends in the market. A technical indicator is a mathematical formula, imputed in trading systems to generate timely buy or sell signals. Technical indicators are generally categorized into two major groups: lagging indicators and leading indicators. Lagging technical indicators are simple moving average, moving average crossover, and AMA′ (Chan, 2018). Simple artificial intelligence methods for time series are discussed for future use. The chapter reviews these techniques to prepare the foundation for the trader to select the trading tool of his choice to begin building a technical trading system in an intelligent manner. A summary of the strengths and weaknesses of existing trading techniques is presented as a conclusion.

Keywords Technical indicators · Simple moving average · Adjustable moving average′ (AMA′) · Artificial intelligence methods for time series

Introduction

Technical indicators are tools of the trade that market technicians use to time and generate trading signals (Edward & Magee, 2008). This chapter reviews the literature on some existing common technical indicators in the

J. Chan, *Automation of Trading Machine for Traders*,
https://doi.org/10.1007/978-981-13-9945-9_2

market. It covers different trading techniques, explaining how they are used to generate timely trading signals. It focuses mainly on a lagging indicator, moving average and explores the ways in which it is used, as trendsetters setters and as breakouts into new trends. The purpose of reviewing these existing techniques is to provide the knowledge foundation for the trader to select the trading tool of his choice to start building technical trading system in the next stage. In conclusion, a summary of the existing techniques and their strengths and weaknesses is presented. This chapter is structured to cover the trading techniques used such as moving averages and its many forms and uses, some breakout methods, and introduction on the uses of artificial intelligence methods in trading.

Technical indicators are trading tools that market technicians use to determine the trends in the market. A technical indicator is a mathematical formula used by traders and is imputed in trading systems to give appropriate buy or sell signals. It can be calculated using past historical prices, and the computed value can be used to anticipate future changes in prices.

Technical indicators are generally categorized into two major groups: lagging indicators and leading indicators. The lagging technical indicators are simple moving average, Moving Average Crossover, and AMA′ (Chan, 2018). In this book, we have also added range breakout models like BBZ (Chan, 2005, 2006) under lagging indicators as they are slower to confirm on the trend than simple moving averages. An example of a leading indicator is Simple Momentum. Another well-known leading indicators is Resistance Strength Index (RSI) (Wilder, 1978).

Lagging Indicators

Lagging indicators are trend-following indicators, which lagged behind the current market. These lagging indicators are characterized by their abilities to perform well in a trending market. During non-trending market condition, that is in a range market, when prices do not exhibit clear direction, often lagging indicators yield false signals which result in small losses.

Simple Moving Average

The best and simplest trading technique is moving average. The basic concept underlying moving average systems is that if the current price is higher than the average price over previous days, there is a possibility of that the current price will continue to climb in a new uptrend.

Moving average is one of the most important lagging technical indicator. Moving average can be viewed as representing the consensus of investors' expectations over a given period. It is simple and easy to calculate and compute. Moving average is the average of a set of numbers that are being averaged continuously while moving through time. Moving average reflects the trend in the price series by smoothing out meaningless fluctuations in the data. In a range trading market, the moving average tends to oscillate sideways. In a trend trading market, the moving average tends to move in a definite upward or downward direction. Therefore, in a trend trading market, the moving average may be used as a technical indicator to give a buy or sell signal.

Simple 20 Day Moving Average (MA20)

The most popular yet simple mechanical trend trading system is the simple moving average used by Brock, Lakonishok, and LeBaron (1992). They demonstrate variable moving average under the rule of SMA (*C*,20,0%), where *C* represents the closing price, 20 is computation of 20 periods moving average, and 0% refers to 0% from the simple moving average. A simple moving average is calculated by adding up the prices for the most recent *n* days and then dividing the sum total by *n*. The number of days (*n*) determines how sensitive the moving average is.

The moving average is computed as follows:

$$\mathrm{SMA}n_t = (1/n)\sum_{i=0}^{n} C_{t-i} \tag{2.1}$$

where SMA is the optimal simple moving average, *n* is 20-day moving average length, and C_t is the closing price at period *t*. When $C_t > \mathrm{SMA}n_t$, the signal is buy long the security, otherwise, sell.

For example, 20-day simple moving average on 30 December 2016 is calculated by adding up all the closes for the last twenty days and dividing by 20 (Table 2.1, Fig. 2.1).

Sell Signal

If the market price is lower than the simple moving average, the market's current expectation can be viewed as being lower than its average expectation over the last *n* days—the market is increasingly bearish. In a trending market, the trading technique when the market price is lower than the simple moving average is to sell.

Table 2.1 CLOF closing prices and moving average

Date	*Closing prices*
02/12/2016	51.68
05/12/2016	51.79
06/12/2016	50.93
07/12/2016	49.77
08/12/2016	50.84
09/12/2016	51.50
12/12/2016	52.83
13/12/2016	52.98
14/12/2016	51.04
15/12/2016	50.90
16/12/2016	51.90
19/12/2016	52.12
20/12/2016	52.23
21/12/2016	52.49
22/12/2016	52.95
23/12/2016	53.02
27/12/2016	53.90
28/12/2016	54.06
29/12/2016	53.77
30/12/2016	53.72
Total	1044.42
Moving average	52.22

Source Author's creation based on CLOF closing prices

Buy Signal

If the market price is higher than the simple moving average, the market's current expectation can be viewed as being higher than its average expectation over the last n days—the market is increasingly bullish. In a trending market, the trading technique when the market price is higher than the simple moving average is to buy.

*Optimized Simple Moving Average (*OptMA*)*

Optimized moving average (OptMA) is the one that is most reflective of the direction of the time series. To obtain OptMA, we need to test all the moving average lengths to choose which one generates the most profit. We can only choose OptMA on hindsight. This OptMA may not be the one that generates profit in the future. Therefore, we use OptMA only if we make the assumption that the future data will be like the past data.

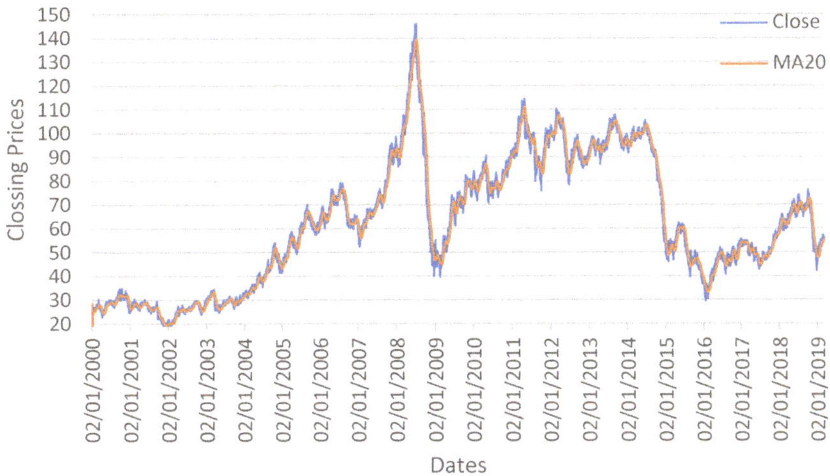

Fig. 2.1 CLOF closing prices and MA20 (*Source* Author's creation based on CLOF closing prices and MA20)

In theory, on hindsight, the most optimized length moving average is the one that produces the most profit. With historical data, this can easily be computed and the most optimized length of the moving average can easily be determined. However, it is not possible to predict which length moving average to would be the most optimal to use in the future. The best that a rational trader can do is to assume that the next day will be like the days in the previous months. This OptMA is used as a benchmark of what an ideal length MA would be, on hindsight.

OptMA is computed in the same way as SMA:

$$\mathrm{SMA}n_t = (1/n)\sum_{i=0}^{n} C_{t-i} \tag{2.2}$$

where SMA is the optimal simple moving average, n is most Optimal moving average length, and C_t is the closing price at period t. If 50-day is the most optimal moving average that generates the most profit after testing all the moving average lengths (say from 2 to 200), then n is 50. When C_t > 50 SMA, the signal is buy long the security, otherwise, sell.

Finding the right number (n) of days for the moving average is the key to achieve the largest win fall of the trading system. Generally, you may try the Fibonacci numbers, 8, 13, 21, and 34. The general rule is to select a number that:

- results in the least number of whipsaws and
- enters and exits the new trends early.

On hindsight, it is very easy and a matter of running a series of backtests, choosing the one that gives the largest and most consistent profit. You can optimize the parameters, giving a range from 2 to 200. Many trading systems like Bloomberg can run the series of tests for you and show you the most profitable trading system/moving average.

For the period 2000–2014, the most profitable simple moving trading system is 50-day moving average (Fig. 2.2).

You can see in the chart that OptMA is almost a perfect fit for most of the years (from 2000 to 2014). However, in later years (2015–2018) and especially 2018, it did not fit as well to the crude light oil futures (CLOF) prices like it did earlier. This is an example of the market's changing behavior.

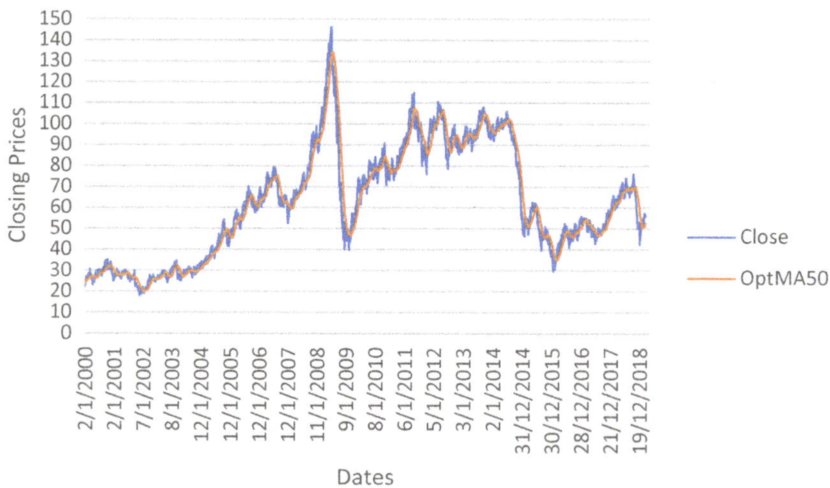

Fig. 2.2 CLOF closing prices and most optimized moving average (MA50) (*Source* Author's creation based on CLOF closing prices and most optimized moving average [MA50])

3- and 21-Day Moving Averages Crossover (MAC 3,21)

Moving averages crossover (MAC) is the short-term moving average crossing over the long-term moving average. The short-term and long-term lengths employed are arbitrary. MAC is known as variable moving average (3,21,0%) in Brock et al. (1992), where 3 refers to the short-term 3-day length MA and 21 refers to 21-day length MA, and 0% refers to 0% MAC is also very popular among practitioners who look for golden cross at lower range to signal the beginning of an uptrend and a dead cross at the upper range to signal the reversal and onset of a new downtrend.

The golden cross is found when the short-term moving average crosses the long-term moving average from the bottom and a buying signal is prompted when SMA3 > SMA21.

The dead cross is formed when the short-term moving average crosses the long-term moving average from the top and the signal becomes a sell signal when SMA3 < SMA21.

Both the moving average lengths, 3 and 21, are the most commonly used ones by market practitioners. Again, optimization can be performed to obtain the most ideal lengths for the moving averages for historical data, but then again, it is not possible to predict the optimal moving averages' lengths that generate the most profit for future use (Fig. 2.3).

A buying signal is prompted when SMA3 > SMA21, a selling signal when otherwise.

The trading rule is:

- Sell (enter short) at 29.61 when 3-day moving average was at 30.77, less than 21-day moving average at 30.83, on 8 February 2016.
- Buy (exit short) at 31.48 when 3-day moving average was at 31.48, more than 21-day moving average at 30.48 on 22 February 2016.

The loss is −$1.79.

To beat the general market masses, some adjustments may be necessary to change these very common techniques into something extraordinary that is suited to trading in your particular market. This adaptation to a local market requires some research into the properties of the price series being traded. After research, fine-tuning of the number of periods for the moving average or standard deviation is required. A shorter number of periods will catch the trend earlier but will result in a lot of false trades in

Fig. 2.3 CLOF closing prices and moving average crossover (MA3 and MA21) (*Source* Author's creation based on CLOF closing prices and moving average crossover [MA3 and MA21])

range trading. A longer number of periods will miss out a larger part of the trend's initial movement but is more confirmed.

Adjustable Moving Average′ (AMA′)

Studies have shown the existence of time-varying volatility in financial and economic time-series data (Gandolfi, Rossolini, Sabatini, & Caselli, 2008). To prevent excessive whipsaws (false entries that result in small losses), adjustable moving average′ (AMA′) is proposed (Chan, 2018). AMA′ varies the length of the moving average according to the market volatilities.

AMA′ uses a ratio (long-term standard deviation over short-term standard deviation) called efficacy ratio to change each period length of the moving average according to the prevailing market volatilities. Efficacy ratio is a time-varying parameter where it adjusts automatically to adapt to the current market condition. Efficacy ratio generates a longer length moving average length when the market moves within a certain trading range for a continuous period of time. It produces a shorter length moving average when the closing prices are trending.

The purpose of proposing efficacy ratio to be incorporated into AMA′ is to generate signals that are sensitive to the directional change and yet will not respond to directionless market movements. The signal is to long the security if C_t> AMA′$_t$. If C_t< AMA′$_t$, then the signal is to short the security.

AMA′ and efficacy ratio are expressed as follows.

$$\text{AMA}'v_t = (1/v)\sum_{i=0}^{v} C_{t-i} \tag{2.3}$$

where ν_t is the efficacy ratio

Efficacy ratio = long-term standard deviation/short-term standard deviation (2.4)

This efficacy ratio (Eq. 2.4) is a time-varying parameter where it is able to adjust automatically according to the current market condition. Efficacy ratio generates a longer moving average length when the market moves within a certain trading range for a continuous period of time. It produces shorter length when the closing prices are trending.

If C_t> AMA′$_t$, then the signal is to buy. If C_t< AMA′$_t$, then the signal is to sell (Fig. 2.4).

The trading rule is:

- Sell (enter short) at the open on 5 January 2016 at 39.09 when the closing price on 4 January 2016 at 38.93 was less than AMA′ at 43.23.
- Buy (exit short) at the open on 28 January 2016 at 34.99 on when the closing price on 27 January 2016 was more than AMA′.

Using the innovated trading rules, this strategy gives a gain of $4.10 from 5 January 2016 to 27 January 2016.

Range Breakout Model

The market is either trading in a range or it has broken out of the range into a trend. The defining moment occurs when it is breaking out of the current range into a new trend. A trading range breakout system, a trading system that emits a signal upon breaking out of the range, is the simplest mechanical trading system.

Fig. 2.4 CLOF closing prices and adjustable moving average′ (AMA′) (*Source* Author's creation based on CLOF closing prices and adjustable moving average′ [AMA′])

In an absolute trading breakout model, when the current price breaks out of the trading range as signified by the last high (or x number of periods high), the trading signal is to buy. When the current price breaks out of the trading range as signified by the last low (or x number of periods low), the trading signal is to sell. A 20-day breakout system is to buy on breakup above the last 20 days trading range and to sell on breakdown below the last 20 days trading range. If the market price is higher than any other prices in the last 20 days, the signal is to buy. If the market price is lower than any other prices in the last 20 days, the signal is to sell. If the market price is still within the 20-day range, volatility is low. There is no volatility breakout. Therefore, in a trend trading system, there is no signal to buy or to sell. If the market price is outside the 20-day range, volatility is high. There is a signal to buy if the market price is higher than the highest price in the last 20 days. There is a signal to sell if the market price is lower than the lowest price in the last 20 days.

Other forms of trading range breakout are breakouts from bands. The bands may be a constant *x*% from the moving average band or they may be standard deviation (volatility) bands.

Fixed Percentage Price Envelope (Moving Average Envelope Band (SMA (1,20,1%)))

Fixed percentage trading bands are sometimes referred to as the moving average envelope. Fixed percentage trading bands are developed from the moving average. The middle band is the moving average; the upper band is the moving average extended upward by *x*%; and the lower band is the moving average extended downwards by *x*%. Moving average envelopes are initially used by Dow theorists to avoid trading (whipsaws) when the moving average is flat (when the market is ranging). Dow theorists use the upper band as a confirmation of the buy signal and the lower band as a confirmation of the sell signal. They do not trade when the market is ranging between the upper band and the lower band. Theoretically, the percentage should be set to encompass all the prices are going nowhere when the market is ranging. If the percentage is set wide enough, the bands should cover most observations.

After the moving average line is drawn, the *x*% of moving average may be calculated and added onto the moving average to form the upper *x*% moving average band and subtracted from the moving average to form the lower *x*% moving average band.

Some novice traders would be tempted to use the upper band as resistance and a possible point to sell and the lower band as support and a possible point to buy. However, on closer observation it can be seen that this strategy does not always make a profit and the potential loss can be huge as there is no inherent, in-built risk control mechanism.

To overcome excess losses brought about by whipsaws in range market, a certain percentage band above and below the moving average is added to confirm the generated signal. In Brock et al. (1992), SMA (1,20,1%) refers to 1% band above and below the 20-day simple moving average. To construct the upper band, 1% is added to the 20-day simple moving average whereas to establish the lower band, 1% is deducted from the 20-day moving average. 1% above the moving average gives additional confirmation of an uptrend while 1% below it confirms the downtrend.

A buy-on-uptrend signal is called upon when the closing price transcends the upper 1% band. An exit long signal is triggered when the closing price returns below the upper 1% band. Vice versa, a sell-on-downtrend signal

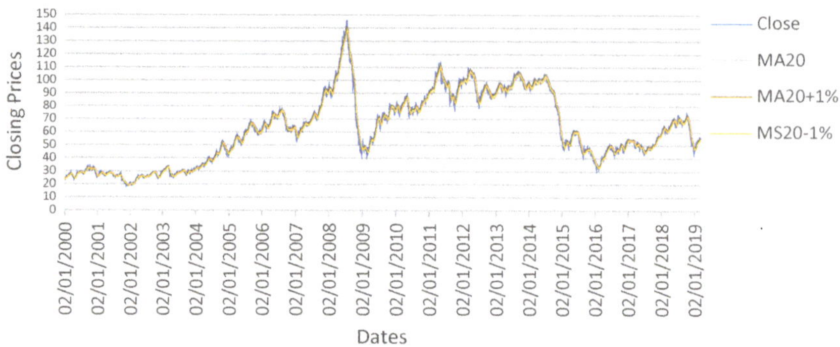

Fig. 2.5 CLOF closing prices and moving average envelope of 1% (*Source* Author's creation based on CLOF closing prices and moving average envelope of 1%)

will prompt when the closing price dips below the lower 1% band and an exit short signal will emerge when that price bounces back above the lower 1% band.

The upper 1% band is calculated as follows:

$$1.01 \times \text{SMA}n_t \tag{2.5}$$

Similarly, the lower 1% band is calculated as follows:

$$0.99 \times \text{SMA}n_t \tag{2.6}$$

where

$$\text{SMA}n_t = (1/n)\sum_{i=0}^{n} C_{t-i} \tag{2.7}$$

A better fit may be to use volatility (standard deviation) to define the trading range (Fig. 2.5).

Standard Deviation Breakout Bands (BBZ)

Volatility may be defined as how prices move in relation to the mean, whether they move far apart from the mean or their movements are very erratic. Statistically, volatility is measured by variance and standard deviation. Variance and standard deviation calculate the possible variations and standard deviations from the mean (average).

The mathematical formula for standard deviation is:

$$\sigma = \sqrt{\sum (x - \overline{x})^2 / n} \quad (2.8)$$

In statistics, if the data are normal, a normal bell-shaped curve would form for the distribution of the frequency of the data. According to statistical theory, about 68% of all observations fall within one standard deviation of the mean and about 95% of all observations fall within two standard deviation. If the distribution does not result in a normal bell shape curve, the data is said to be abnormal. In technical analysis, a two-standard deviation band system was created by John Bollinger (2002) for use as a technical tool.

If the returns from a certain trading strategy result in fat tails distribution, then the returns are higher than expected of a random distribution. There is a possibility that the returns from using the particular technical indicator are better than the passive buy and hold strategy.

The standard deviation bands (BBZ) breakout technique is to use the standard deviations from the moving average instead of fixed percentage like 1%.

If the trend trader can identify the beginning of trends to trade, then he can profit by riding on the trend. One of the methods using standard deviation band is to identify the trading range and then trade when price is out of the small trading range. Therefore, instead of using 2 standard deviations, 1 standard deviation may be another alternative to consider. When the price is above the upper 1 standard deviation band, the strategy is to buy long. When the price returns to trade within the bands, the strategy is to exit long by selling.

For futures, when short is allowed, the strategy would be to sell short when price falls below the lower 1 standard deviation band and to exit short when the price reenters the lower 1 standard deviation band. A break above the 1 standard deviation from the moving average constitutes a buy signal for trend traders like me where an uptrend begins after breaking out of the congested trading range band. Similarly, a sell signal emerges upon breaking down from the −1 (minus one) standard deviation band from the moving average.

Do not take within the bands. Note that the trends above and below the bands last longer and thus profits are larger. The whipsaws that result are very small in comparison.

As professional traders, we are not interested in low returns. We are only interested in high returns, which are usually accompanied by high risk (as measured by high volatility). Volatility is high when the market is out of range trading; when it is trend trading. The trading technique therefore is to buy on breakup of a range as defined by the one standard deviation upper band and to sell on breakdown of a range as defined by the one standard deviation lower band.

If the price breaks above the standard deviation, it is a buy signal. If it breaks below the −1 standard deviation, it is a sell signal.

These simple trading techniques can be drafted into what some traders call trading rules:

- Buy (enter long) when prices are more than one standard deviation ($P >$ upper band).
- Sell (exit long) when prices are less than one standard deviation ($P <$ upper band).
- Sell (enter short) when prices are less than minus one (−1) standard deviation ($P <$ lower band).
- Buy (exit short) when prices are more than minus one (−1) standard deviation ($P >$ lower band).

A trading example using BBZ (20-day standard deviation bands) can be conducted to confirm that it is profitable. Using the simple trading rules of selling below the lower −1 standard deviation band and buying back above the lower −1 standard deviation band, this strategy gives a $3.84 gain from 5 January 2016 to 22 January 2016.

Note that with this technique you enter later than the moving average on more confirmation and exit earlier than the moving average (Fig. 2.6).

Sell (enter short) at the open on 6 January 2016 at 38.46 when the closing price on 5 January 2016 at 38.23 was less than the −1 standard deviation lower band at 38.44.

Buy (exit short) at the open on 25 January 2016 at 34.62 when the closing price on 22 January 2016 at 34.67 more than the −1 standard deviation lower band at 34.07.

The profit is 3.84.

This is the basis of some mathematical trading models. The weakness of volatility breakout systems is they only work for the market when it is

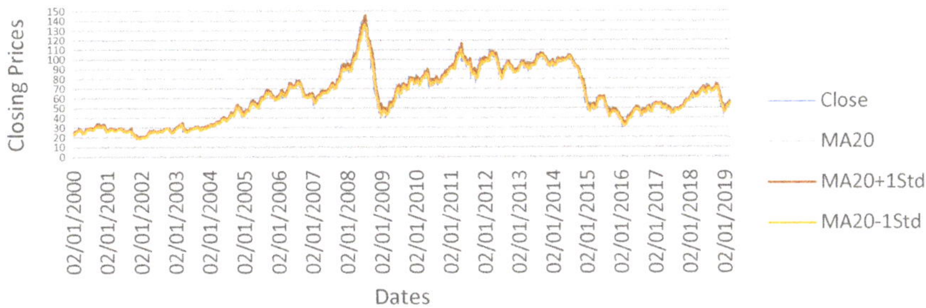

Fig. 2.6 CLOF closing prices and BBZ (*Source* Author's creation based on CLOF closing prices and BBZ)

trending. When the market is ranging, the trading systems generate a lot of false trading signals.

Leading Indicators

Leading indicators are technical indicators that predict if the market is overbought or oversold. They are used to anticipate overbought market condition near the resistance to generate a mechanical sell signal and similarly, they generate a buy signal when they perceive that market is near support level. Therefore, the knowledge of anticipated resistance and support is important to gauge where the areas where range traders consider the market as oversold or overbought.

Therefore, leading indicators provide useful signals during this range market condition. However, leading indicators generally experience huge losses in a trending market. In range trading, the trading technique is to sell at the area of resistance and buy at the area of support.

An example of a leading indicator is an oscillator. Oscillator is a leading indicator based on momentum. Momentum is the rate of change.

Momentum

The simplest momentum calculation is the difference between today's close and the close n days ago as a percentage of the daily return. Graphically, this can be depicted by a horizontal median also called the equilibrium line. When the current price is higher than the price n days ago, the momentum is above the equilibrium line. When the momentum is above the equilibrium line and rising, prices are advancing with increasing momentum. An extreme momentum reading above the equilibrium line indicates an overbought level. When the current price is lower than the price n days ago, the momentum is below the equilibrium and if it is falling, then prices are falling with increasing momentum. An extreme momentum reading below the equilibrium line indicates an oversold level. As with moving averages, the number of days, *n*, used in an oscillator determines how sensitive the indicator will be.

Other leading indicators like Stochastics (Lane, 1982), RSI, and Directional Movement Index (DMI) by Wilder (1978), work on similar concept.

Conclusion: The Key to Model Trading Is the Inherent Technical Indicator

It is up to the individual trader to find the technical indicator(s) that suit(s) him or her and the markets being traded. The chosen technical indicator depends on where the traders' expected return and the level of risk of loss the trader can tolerate. It also depends on the particular markets that the trader chooses. The particular market that the trader chooses must also commensurate with his or her desired return and risk appetite.

In this chapter, we explored and examined some of the popular and useful technical indicators such as moving averages and standard deviations. In the next chapter, we will first research the markets to test the profitability of trading rules employing the popular technical indicators.

Review

- The main weaknesses of the moving average are that: It is a lagging indicator so turning points will always lag behind the corresponding transition in the current price series, and while it tends to do well in a trending market, it generates a lot of false signals in a range market.
- Some trend traders prefer to take a holiday during a range market to avoid these whipsaws. A range market usually happens when the moving average is flattish.
- You may use several moving averages to determine if the market is in a range or you may use envelope bands around the moving average to define range trading areas.

- Trading range breakout is a trading strategy to buy when the current price breaks up above a certain trading range and to sell when the current price breaks down below a certain trading range.
- The simplest trading range breakout is when the current price moves above the previous x period high or below the previous x period low.
- Another way to define trading range is as a constant x% from the moving average. This covers most observations. However, the range area is wide and does not fit the data set well.
- A better fit to the data set would be Bollinger bands. These are two standard deviations from the 20-day moving average. Two standard deviations cover 95.5% of all observations in a normal distribution.
- However, this is not helpful in mechanical trading decision making because two standard deviations define a relative high and low and require other indicators for confirmation.
- Therefore, a smaller trading range would be one standard deviation which, if it is a normal distribution, would cover 68% of all observations.
- A mechanical trading buy or sell signal would occur above +1 or below −1 standard deviations.
- The shorter moving average has narrower bands and results in quicker earlier entry and more whipsaws. This is why the shorter moving average and standard deviation work for a trending market.
- The longer moving average has broader bands and results in slower entry and fewer whipsaws. This is why a longer moving average and standard deviation work to avoid ranging markets.
- The weaknesses of oscillators as technical indicators for a trading system are that because oscillators are predictive and are not as reliable as historical prices or lagging indicators, like moving averages, which try to confirm the trend, they give signals at the first signs of divergence and sometimes the signals proved to be false.
- Therefore, the weakness in volatility breakout systems is that they do not work in range trading as they generate a lot of false trading signals.
- New trading systems like adjustable moving average′ (AMA′) can help to make the size of the moving average more flexible to suit the prevailing market condition.
- Last word: The concept of mathematical formulas for technical indicators is very good and is a good habit to adopt as we design, construct, and test technical indicators for mechanical trading systems.

References

Bollinger, J. (2002). *Bollinger on Bollinger*. New York: McGraw Hill.

Brock, W., Lakonishok, J., & LeBaron, B. (1992, December). Simple technical trading rules and the stochastic properties of stock returns. *Journal of Finance, 47*(5), 1731–1764.

Chan, J. (2005, March/April). Using time series volatilities to trade trends: Trading technique—BBZ. *Australian Technical Analysts Association Journal*, 31–38.

Chan, J. (2006, March). Trading trends with the Bollinger bands Z-test. *Technical Analysis of Stocks & Commodities*, 46–52.

Chan Phooi M'ng, J. (2018). Dynamically adjustable moving average′ (AMA′) technical analysis indicator to forecast Asian Tigers' futures markets. *Physica A: Statistical Mechanics and Its Applications, 509*, 336–345.

Edwards, R. D., & Magee, J. (2008). *Technical analysis of stock trends* (9th ed.). Chicago, IL: John Magee Inc.

Lane, G. (1982). Lane's stochastic. *Traders' Magazine*.

Gandolfi, G., Rossolini, M., Sabatini, A., & Caselli, S. (2008). Dynamic MACD standard deviation embedded in MACD indicator for accurate adjustment to financial market dynamics. *International Federation of Technical Analysts Journal*, 16–23.

Wilder, W. (1978). *New concepts in technical trading systems*. New York: Trend Research.

CHAPTER 3

Market Data Analysis

Abstract Data analysis reveals the empirical properties of market prices. Traders use descriptive data statistics to find the most lucrative market and financial instrument to trade. This chapter explores the characteristics of markets, and it concentrates on futures contracts, where the trader is able to short sell the market. Traded on margin, futures are attractively leveraged. This chapter focuses on data analysis methodology and deciphering empirical properties of financial instruments with the objective of applying the evidence and results to develop trading systems that yield high returns at low, controlled risks. The conclusion from this chapter is that from data analysis, empirical properties of the financial time series can be observed and appropriate dynamic adaptive trading models can be built to suit the chosen time series.

Keywords Financial market data analysis · Descriptive data statistics · Futures contracts · Dynamic adaptive trading model

Introduction

Before any trader attempts to enter any market, he must do his own research. The first and important step in research is to analyze the price time series to detect and recognize repeating patterns for the purpose of understanding market and price behaviors. Therefore, this chapter explores

J. Chan, *Automation of Trading Machine for Traders*,
https://doi.org/10.1007/978-981-13-9945-9_3

the characteristics of the markets and financial instruments. It concentrates on futures, where the trader is able to short sell the market. Another exciting feature inherent in futures is it is highly leveraged as it is traded on margin. Therefore, it is very important to understand the nature of futures contracts before any trader attempts to trade it.

The purpose of data analysis is to study the empirical properties of the price behaviors of the market that the trader is interested in trading. The objective of data analysis is to find the most lucrative markets and financial instruments to trade. With this knowledge of the characteristics of the market and price behaviors, the ultimate aim of this book of developing the most suitable and effective algorithm technical trading system can be achieved to harvest the maximum profit from the most lucrative markets.

This chapter emphasizes the empirical properties of a market and price time series with the objective of applying the evidence and results to develop and test trading systems that yield high returns at low, controlled risks. It covers the methodology of data analysis for time series data.

Choosing the Markets to Trade

The different markets can be the foreign exchange, equity, commodity, and futures markets. Different markets will have different behaviors, different mean returns, standard deviations, and kurtosis for different financial instruments have different kind of returns and risks. Choosing the markets to trade may be the most difficult decision for some. If the decision is based on some criteria, it may be a very easy choice. If the criteria set for the trend trader is the largest expected return (mean of the return) at the least risk (standard deviation), it is a simple task to do descriptive statistics on all the assets and select the one(s) that gives the highest expected return per unit of standard deviation. The assumption here is that the particular chosen market will continue to behave in the near future like the way it had been behaving the last one to ten years. Besides the mean, the other statistics that the trend trader is interested in is the kurtosis of the asset's time series. A fat tail at the end of the distribution promises fat returns.

Different markets are dominated by different types of traders and different needs as determined by supply and demand factors. Thus, each market has its own peculiar characteristic. The trading in major currencies foreign exchange is fast and furious whereas money market is dominated by large institutions and huge volume trading. Futures contracts are derived from the underlying assets and yet possess much higher risk. Stock futures contracts possess much higher risk of percentage loss than stocks because of the leverage factor attributed to trading on margin at a fraction of the contract size. The peculiar characteristic of the particular market determines the technical indicators to use.

Literature review on technical analysis finds that currencies appear to be the most popular studies (Irwin & Park, 2009; Olson, 2004). Most of the studies conclude that the trading experience with currencies is positive (Menkhoff & Taylor, 2006; Taylor & Allen, 1992). However, Olson (2004) points out that, in general, technical trading strategies for currencies were profitable until the early 1990s but have not been since then. Stock markets appear to be the second most popular study (Lukac, Brorsen, & Irwin, 1988, 1990). Interestingly, Dow Jones Industrial Average stocks, which were profitable earlier, failed to make as many profits after 1990 and new emerging markets show greater potential for profit-making using common technical analysis tools like moving averages.

Futures markets appear to be least researched. Most of the studies show consistent profits across most of the indices and commodities futures. Generally, studies (Olson, 2004) show that profits are less in sophisticated and mature markets such as foreign exchange and the stock exchanges of major financial centers. Generally, from the review of past studies, most tests show positive net returns over the last 2 decades in the different commodity and financial markets. Although earlier studies did not take into account transaction costs for the equities and futures markets (Irwin & Park, 2009), the studies after 1990 still show positive net returns after covering transaction costs.

Exchange-traded futures involve a standard contract to buy or sell a specific underlying asset, whether this is a theoretical basket of stocks or a fixed amount of a commodity such as crude light oil, sometime in the future. Futures contracts are standardized according to contract specifications which include:

- the underlying asset;
- the contract value and minimum tick;
- the contract months and expiry dates;
- cash settlement or cash delivery.

For example, the contract specifications of Crude Light Oil traded on Chicago Mercantile Exchange Group (CME Group).

- The underlying asset is crude light oil.
- The contract unit is 1000 barrels.
- The price quotation is US Dollars (USD) and Cents per barrel.
- The minimum price fluctuation is $0.01 per barrel.
- The contract months are consecutive months listed for the first five years.
- The settlement method is deliverable which means that if the seller has to deliver 1000 barrels of crude light oil on the maturity date to the buyer.

Futures are traded on margins, which means the trader has to pay only a fraction of the contract size for guarantee of the performance of the contract. The margin of most futures ranges between 5 and 20% of contract size, based on the clearing house's calculation of the volatility of historical prices. If the margin for Crude Light Oil Futures (CLOF) is $2700, then at 39.09, the margin will be almost 7%. Futures are highly leveraged and can greatly enhance the portfolio performance if they are profitable. They can cause financial ruin if the transaction results in great loss. This can be why some people regard futures as a dangerous financial instrument. Professional traders regard futures as one of the best instruments to trade because of very high returns.

Using the innovated AMA′ of selling (enter short) at the open on 5 January 2016 at 39.09 and exiting short at the open on 28 January 2016 at 34.99, gives a gain of $4.10.

If the contract value of one CLOF futures contract is 39.09 × $10 × 100 = $39,090, and the margin is $2700, the trader only deposits with the futures broker about 7% of the actual contract size.

If the trading profit before transaction costs is 4.10 × $1000 = $4100 and the margin paid is $2700, the return is huge at 152%.

This book uses CLOF contract for illustration purposes because it is one of the most traded commodities futures. It also had one of the highest mean per unit of standard deviation.

Descriptive Statistics

In research, the first step is to perform data analysis and know basic descriptive statistics such as the mean, standard deviation, skewness, and kurtosis for returns. The kurtosis is descriptive statistic that is of most important to a trend trader who looks for fat tails that have kurtoses much higher than the normal 3. The fat tails on either end promise fat returns to trend traders. The main characteristic in time series that traders are interested in is volatility or huge returns which are found in the heavy tails of the daily price changes' distributions.

Fama (1965) states that two ways to test for trends in the market are:

1. Common statistical tools such as serial correlation coefficient and analyses of runs of consecutive price changes of the same sign.
2. Mechanical trading rules or charting techniques, based solely on patterns in the past history of price changes, which can make profits greater than with a naive buy-and-hold policy.

The purpose of statistical tests, therefore, is to check if they support the assumption of independence. If they do not conclusively support this assumption, then the next step is to proceed with testing mechanical trading rules based on patterns in the past price history for expected profits greater than those of the naive buy-and-hold policy.

The raw historical data on the open, high, low, close, volume, and open interest can be collected from sources like Bloomberg and Thompson Reuters. The daily closing prices for CME's CLOF are collected from Bloomberg for the period 2 January 2000 to 31 December 2018. The purpose of data and preliminary analysis is to examine the volatility of the returns of these oil futures.

The descriptive statistics in Table 3.1 show that the average daily returns for CLOF 0.04% and the standard deviation is 2.04%. The skewness is −0.27 and the kurtosis is 5.14. These statistics validate that this time series is not normally distributed and displays leptokurtic characteristic. It can be inferred that CLOF prices are not random. The kurtosis of this distribution of 5.14 is higher than that of the normal distribution. The data analysis ascertains that the presence of fat tails and the hypothesis is to test for fat returns using dynamically adaptive technical trading system.

Table 3.1 Descriptive statistics of CLOF

	CLOF (%)
Mean	0.04
Median	0.11
Maximum	8.93
Minimum	−10.05
Std. dev.	2.04
Skewness	−0.27
Kurtosis	5.14

Source Author's creation based on CLOF closing prices

Conclusion: You Need a Positive Statistical Expectation Edge for Your Trading Strategy

Finding the positive statistical expectation edge for your trading may be as simple as finding the average daily return and daily standard deviation within a month, a quarter, or a year, similar to checking for fat tail distributions. The fatter the tails, the bigger the potential profits and the more lucrative the markets for you to trade. Some futures contracts, like CLOF, and the stock indices futures contracts of emerging markets are among the best markets to trade because of the leverage factor.

The data analysis ascertains that volatility of CLOF prices appears in clusters. These observations infer that the prices of CLOF display dynamic variance characteristic and therefore require a trading model that is dynamic in nature.

Review

- Before any trader attempts to enter any market, he must do his own research. The first and important step in research is to analyze the price time series to detect and recognize repeating patterns for the purpose of understanding market and price behaviors.
- The purpose of data analysis is to study the empirical properties of the price behaviors of the market that the trader is interested in trading.
- The objective of data analysis is to find the most lucrative markets and financial instruments to trade.

- In research, the first step is to perform data analysis and know basic statistics such as the mean, standard deviation, skewness, and kurtosis for returns.
- Different markets will have different characteristics; it is important to specialize in finding the right technical indicator that can decipher the peculiarity of the particular market.
- Futures market appears to be the least researched studies, and most of the studies appear to show consistent profits across most of the indices and commodities futures.
- Fama (1965) states that two ways to test for trends in the market are:
  - Common statistical tools such as serial correlation coefficient and analyses of runs of consecutive price changes of the same sign.
  - Mechanical trading rules or charting techniques, based solely on patterns in the past history of price changes, which can make profits greater than with a naive buy-and-hold policy.
- The purpose of statistical tests, therefore, is to check if they support the assumption of independence. If they do not conclusively support this assumption, then the next step is to proceed with testing mechanical trading rules based on patterns in the past price history for expected profits greater than those of the naive buy-and-hold policy.

References

Fama, E. (1965). Random walks in stock market prices. *Financial Analyst Journal, 16,* 1–16.

Irwin, S., & Park, C. (2009). A reality check on technical trading rule profits in the U.S. futures markets. *Journal of Futures Markets, 30,* 633–659.

Lukac, L., Brorsen, B., & Irwin, S. (1988). Similarity of computer guided technical trading systems. *Journal of Futures Markets, 8*(1–13), 64.

Lukac, L., Brorsen, B., & Irwin, S. (1990). *A comparison of twelve technical trading systems.* Greenville, SC: Traders Press.

Menkhoff, L., & Taylor, M. P. (2006). *The obstinate passion of foreign exchange professionals: Technical analysis.* (Warwick Economics Research Paper 872), 870–912.

Olson, D. (2004). Have trading rule profits in the currency markets declined over time? *Journal of Banking & Finance, 28,* 85–105.

Taylor, M., & Allen, H. (1992). The use of technical analysis in the foreign exchange market. *Journal of International Money and Finance, 11*(3), 304–314.

CHAPTER 4

Development of Technical Algorithm Trading Systems

Abstract Technical trading systems consist of sets of trading rules, selected after series of rigorous tests to generate timely trading signals. Algorithmic trading works well on the basic principle of employing the most suitable algorithm to the prevailing market condition, automatically executing appropriate trading signals via a computer program. This research develops an adjustable moving average′ (AMA′) into an algorithm trading system that market professionals can use on model trading desks. This chapter continues with development and tests of AMA′. It identifies and suggests ways to overcome some common problems inherent in traditional trading systems. It depicts the profile of an ideal algorithm trend trading system. This chapter methodologically tests trading systems for the purpose of developing one that yields high returns at low, controlled risks.

Keywords Technical trading system · Trading rules · Algorithmic trading · Model trading desk

Introduction

Algorithm trading systems involve using mechanical technical trading rules. Algorithm trading is completely automated; thus, it is also known at robo trading. It is also called algo trading and black box trading. The most

J. Chan, *Automation of Trading Machine for Traders*,
https://doi.org/10.1007/978-981-13-9945-9_4

general principle of algorithm trading is employing an algorithm that is suitable to the prevailing market condition and automatically executing the trading signal via a computer program. The algorithm is selected after intensive backtesting, optimization, and out-of-sample test. An algorithm trading system is used because historically it has been tested and proven to have a statistical edge in generating positive abnormal returns above the buy-and-hold policy.

The technical trading system basically consists of a set of trading rules selected after a series of tests, to generate trading signals. The trading rules consist of algorithms with optimized parameters to indicate trading signals. The trading signal is either long or short a contract. Therefore, this research develops from a set of trading rules on adjustable moving average to become an algorithm trading system that professional market technicians can use on the model trading desk.

Market statistics gave hints as to the market's characteristics (as discussed in the previous chapter), and this chapter tests the relevant trading rules that can decipher prominent trends in that market and discusses how to put the appropriate trading rules together into a trading system.

This chapter describes some common problems inherent in traditional trend trading systems and suggests ways to overcome these common problems. It depicts the profile of an ideal algorithm trend trading system. This chapter looks at the methodology to test trading systems for the purpose of developing one that yields high returns at low, controlled risks.

Learning to design an algorithm trading system is one of the first subjects undertaken by an apprentice trader to become a professional market technician working in the model trading desk of a financial institution. The professional market technician is trading according to some proprietary algorithm trading system which is not readily available in the market. This trading system is developed by the market technician for his own trading use. It is highly unlikely that he will share his trading system with the public.

Profile of an Algorithm Trend Trading System

The use of a well-defined algorithm trading system is very important to the financial institution which has house proprietary trading operation. The choice and implementation of an algorithm trading system can be the defining factor to determine the overall profit or loss of the financial institution for each accounting period.

Normally, a quantitative trader uses an algorithm trading system to generate automated buying and selling in the markets that he has tested. Therefore, algorithm trading system involves not only signal generation but also automated stop loss. There is no allowance for human judgment or interference.

Although the primary objective of a defined algorithm trading system is to generate excess abnormal return, the function of the defined algorithm trading system also helps to prevent uncontrollable large trading losses which may cause the collapse of the financial institution.

The benefit of using an algorithm trading system is all trading decisions are objective and quantifiable, which means that every trade can be accounted for by the algorithm when audited. This ensures that all trades, profits, and losses are systematic, with no drastic, unexpected huge losses of gigantic nature compared to its paid-up capital. All losses are expected.

An adjustable algorithm trading system is defined as an automated trading system that can adjust its parameters instantly to adapt to the current market condition. The special feature of an adaptive algorithm trading system is its ability to automatically adjust its parameter to become a large variable in range trading period, and to become a small variable in trend trading period. The technical trading system functions according to the inherent algorithm which first recognizes the state the market is in, ranging or trending, and then adjusts the parameters accordingly. Flexible trading systems that can adjust its parameters automatically to changes in market conditions may be the area of future development for algorithmic trading.

Besides being robust, a trading system is used to gain a statistical edge, objectivity, and consistency. A robust trading system is defined as one that can withstand a variety of market conditions across many markets and timeframes. The trader can trade in timeframes of seconds, minutes (five, 10, 15, 30), hourly, daily, and weekly. It is rare to find a trader who uses a monthly or yearly timeframe because trends happen within the month and the majority of the profit would have been missed on monthly confirmation.

Two market conditions that are important to traders are:

- Range market when the price movements are small and many, which result in small gains for the range trader and small losses for the trend trader.

- Trend market when there is a large price movement, which results in a huge gain for the trend trader and a huge loss for the range trader.

Therefore, generally most traders would prefer trading in a trend market. The trading system must be backtested and tested live (in line with out-of-sample testing) to withstand these two very different market conditions and the results of these tests must be positive. The trading system must have a positive expectation. The most important reason to use a trading system is to gain a statistical edge. This statistical edge also refers to the probability of ruin. The smaller the probability of ruin, the more likely the trader survives and profits from the trading system in the long run.

A good, flexible, algorithm trend trading system that is robust and has a statistical positive expectation edge should aim to be tested according to the following criteria:

1. A well thought out design that uses appropriate technical analysis tools. The potential stop loss, if placed at the moving average or standard deviation levels, is relatively small. This is part of the reason why we have selected moving average as a technical indicator tool to be incorporated into our trading system.
2. Parameters that have been tested to fit historical price data must fit future price movement. Selecting a parameter based on historical data is easy, because optimization is simply a matter of choosing the highest net profit at the lowest maximum consecutive loss. The assumption made here is that the future price movements are repetitions of present and past price movements. As this may or may not be the case and some fine-tuning is required, it is preferable if the trading system incorporates an algorithm that performs this fine-tuning and optimization automatically.
3. A good trading system is robust across most markets in any time-frame. A trend trading system tends to do better with daily data but in fast, volatile markets a daytrader may apply the trading system after rigorous testing. After adjusting for the parameters to suit the current prevailing market, the trading system should be robust enough to be traded on any market, be it equity, commodity, or financial futures market.
4. High profits to low risk ratios. The total accumulated profits net of all transaction costs compared with the total accumulated losses

of the trading system give this reward to risk ratio. The higher this ratio, the better the trading system is. As a rule of thumb, this ratio should be at the very least more than 1.5.

5. Number of winning trades that are about equal to, or more than, losing trades. Over the long run, on average at any point in time there is a 50% chance that the price will go up and a 50% chance that it will go down. At the point of entry, the chance of the trade being a winning trade is also 50%. So, if on average, the number of winning trades that the trading system generates is 50%, this should be good enough.
6. Average gain is much larger than average loss. If the chances of winning and losing are the same, the determining factor must be the winning amount. The average gain must be at least 1.5 times larger than the average loss.
7. Capital preservation and low maximum drawdown with an inherent loss control mechanism. The level of drawdown, the maximum consecutive losses that affect the level of capital, determines if an individual can make it as a professional trader. The loss control mechanism is simply a stop-loss order. According to the trading plan, the stop-loss level must be placed at about one-third of the potential reward. Technically, the stop-loss level must be placed at a point where it will not be triggered unnecessarily. Try to place your stop at uncommon areas where the flood of similar orders will not trigger your stop unnecessarily before the market continues to move in the direction of your position.
8. Ability to avoid some of the whipsaws in a range trading market.
9. Trend trading systems share the common problem of suffering whipsaws in a ranging market. The challenge here is to build an algorithm trading system that can avoid some of the whipsaws in a range trading market. We propose to use a longer moving average in range trading.
10. Ability to enter a new trend early. A tighter band will allow earlier entry. We propose using a shorter moving average when the market starts to trend.
11. Ability to automatically adjust or fine-tune to trend versus range market conditions. The trading system must incorporate an algorithm that automatically adjusts the moving average length to be shorter term when the market starts to trend and be longer term when the market is ranging.

All trading systems have problems. Trend trading systems have problems that are specific to them. There are too many similar trend trading systems that generate similar kinds of orders, thus creating false signals when there are no real trends. Trend trading systems also suffer a lot of whipsaws when the market is ranging. The fast trend trading systems tend to exit the market too early and thus do not capture most of the major price movements while the slow trend trading systems fail to enter the market early and miss large portions of major price movements, especially when prices move unexpectedly and sharply. Most of the time, the trading system parameters have to be fine-tuned to meet current market conditions.

The adjustable algorithm technical trading systems aim to address some of these common problems by automatically adjusting the parameters to cater for different market states, ranging or trending.

Adjustable Moving Average′ (AMA′) uses Efficacy Ratio to change the parameter of the moving average according to the changing market condition. When the market is ranging, Efficacy Ratio dictates a longer moving average, while in trending market, the short suggests using a shorter moving average to enter the new trend earlier.

To sum up, the most important feature of an algorithm trading system is its ability to adapt quickly and be robust in all markets and across time. In designing a new algorithm trading system, the technical indicator used should show this ability.

The objective of the game is to maximize profits while minimizing the risk of losses.

Adjustable Moving Average′ (AMA′)

The main rationale behind using the moving-average rule is that it provides a means of determining the general direction or trend of a market by smoothing out unnecessary noise (Andrada-Felix & Fernandez-Rodriguez, 2008). This is especially meaningful for time-series prices, which are nonlinear because moving-average rules could capture information ignored by their linear counterparts (Gencay & Stengos, 1998; Kwon & Kish, 2002). Gencay and Stengos (1998), use moving average as the prime technical indicator as moving average filters out market noise and captures important information from the nonlinear characteristic of price changes. Since basic technical analysis methods have encountered their limitations, technical analysis as a science has also evolved to include algorithmic trading methods. AMA′ is more suitable than the classical simple moving averages to the ever-changing behavior of the markets.

Consistently predicting the trend accurately from range trading is the most persistent trading problem common to all traders; for applying trend trading rules in ranging markets will result in whipsaws losses and vice versa. The traditional trading rule method like simple fixed-length moving average cannot change to adjust to the varying volatility clustering characteristic that exists in many financial markets. Therefore, with the dynamically changing market volatility, automatic adjustable trading algorithms are more powerful instruments to differentiate trend from range trading. At present, many futures markets experience similar market characteristic where they are ever-changing and new trading systems that adjust in tandem with the prevailing market condition are needed. AMA′ adapts better to the current market condition to cater to the time-varying volatility characteristic of the time series.

Gandolfi, Rossolini Sabatini, and Caselli (2008) address time-varying volatilities in their study by employing an excess "volatility" technical indicator—the ratio of the 10-day standard deviation of closing prices to the 50-day standard deviation of closing prices—in order to determine the weights used in their innovative trading system. Azizan, Mohamed, and Chan Phooi M'ng (2011a, b) employ a ratio of the 34-day standard deviation of closing prices to the 6-day standard deviation of closing prices to determine the length of the moving average used in their trading system, the Adjustable Bands Z-Test (ABZ′). Using the same concept, this paper introduces the Efficacy Ratio (the ratio of the most optimized parameter, *n*, divided by its square-root), to determine the appropriate length of AMA′ suitable to the prevailing trend in different periods (Chan Phooi M'ng, 2018). The value of n is determined from the training in-sample period and employed in the out-of-sample period to determine the most suitable AMA′s length to generate appropriate trading signal in a timely manner.

Unlike conventional methods, AMA′ automatically generates adaptive parameter to fit historical and current data. AMA′ captures a larger portion of the trend and, ultimately, greater abnormal profits by routinely adjusting the parameter according to prevailing market condition, whether ranging or trending. This is consistent with recent findings that statistical learning methods have produced better out-of-sample results than most single and fixed moving-average rules (Lo, Mamaysky, & Wang, 2000).

AMA′ is tested and developed, evolving around the concept of adjusting the moving averages and standard deviations accordingly to an Efficacy Ratio.

AMA′ is timely as it can adjust the trading rule in response to prevailing volatility condition. AMA′ changes each period length of the moving average according to the prevailing Efficacy Ratio. Efficacy Ratio uses a ratio of 50-day standard deviation (for the long-term indicator) over $\sqrt{}$50-day standard deviation (for the short-term indicator).

$$EffR = \frac{LT\sigma}{ST\sigma} \tag{4.1}$$

where *EffR* represents the Efficacy Ratio, while $LT\sigma$ is long-term standard deviation and $ST\sigma$ denotes as short-term standard deviation. This study proposes to use a ratio of 50-day $LT\sigma$ and $\sqrt{}$50-day for $ST\sigma$. The underlying concept of this algorithm, Efficacy Ratio is, it dynamically and automatically varies the parameter of technical indicator to suit the current market condition. This adaptability potentially addresses the most important common problem encountered by traders in gauging whether the market is ranging or beginning to trend.

AMA′ changes the length of the moving average each period according to the prevailing Efficacy Ratio as follows:

$$AMA'_t = \left(\frac{1}{EffR}\right)\sum_{i=0}^{\nu} C_{t-i} \tag{4.2}$$

where *EffR* is the Efficacy Ratio.

The innovation to this moving average makes it adaptive to the current market state, for it to decipher between trend period and range period. The objective of this is to find market anomalies; the hypothesis of excess returns above the threshold buy-and-hold in the long run holds true.

Efficacy Ratio functions to automatically:

1. increase the length of the moving average when the market ranges and
2. decrease the length of the moving average when the market trends.

Tests and Trading Results of Trading Rules

Efficacy Ratio which is incorporated into AMA′, is rigorously tested, validated and monitored using different futures contracts in different time frames before it is documented and considered ready for use by the professional model trading desk. Besides AMA′, we will test the benchmark OptMA and other moving averages and bands.

The technical indicators tested are the ones we discussed earlier in Chapter 2, which are:

1. 20-day Simple Moving Average (SMA20);
2. Moving Average Crossover (MAC);
3. Moving Average Envelope Bands;
4. BBZ;
5. OptMA_n; and
6. AMA′.

This study thus adopts a similar testing approach based on the technical trading rules specified by Lukac, Brorsen, and Irwin (1988) and Brock, Lakonishok, and LeBaron (1992) and others who followed Brock et al. (1992) like Bessembinder and Chan (1998) and Kwon and Kish (2002), which are fixed and variable-lengths moving-average rules.

Hence, this study tests if with the technical rules like simple moving average and MAC used by Lukac et al. (1988) and Brock et al. (1992), produce consistent profits for crude light oil futures (CLOF) markets both in in-sample and out-of-sample periods.

The summed return of this trading rule can be calculated by the following equation and used as a comparison scale among the models and markets:

$$\text{Return}\ (\%) = 100 \times \left(\sum_{t=1}^{b} \left(\frac{y_{t+1} - y_t}{y_t} \right) + \sum_{t=1}^{s} \left(\frac{y_t - y_{t+1}}{y_t} \right) \right) \tag{4.3}$$

where b denotes the total number of long positions and s represents the total number of short positions.

To test the performance of AMA′ trading system, the trading results of AMA′ are evaluated against 4 common trading systems and that of the passive buy-and-hold strategy. The aim here is to test if the mean return of

AMA′ is significantly higher than the other 4 common trading systems and that of the buy-and-hold after transaction costs.

In life trading, transaction costs account for a chunk of the trading losses and thus, it would unrealistic if transaction costs are not included. The transaction cost accounts for brokerage commission including exchange and clearing fees as well as slippage. Therefore, the transaction costs for two ways for CLOF are USD4.60[1] (0.005 of USD0.01 × 10 contract size). Even after taking transaction costs of 0.005 for each CLOF transaction, the trading results confirm AMA′ outperforms the threshold buy-and-hold as well as the 4 tested trading systems.

The base price of $23.87 for CLOF as at the opening of 2 January 2000 is used. The net percentage cumulative returns after transaction costs and 1 tick slippage are computed by taking the gains/losses as percentages of the base price. Table 4.1 depicts the net percentage returns after transaction costs.

The benchmark for any model is that the returns must surpass those of the passive strategy of buy-and-hold (Fama, 1965). The excess return is termed as abnormal return. If the strategy can outperform the benchmark buy-and-hold for different periods of time, then the market prices are not random (Fama, 1965).

Abnormal Returns

The results of these tests are recorded and compared. All the profit results are reported net of transaction costs. AMA's results which are more profitable as it can automatically adjust to shifts in parameter. The following notes summarize the six technical trading rules, including AMA′ and OptMA which is obtained after a series of backtesting exercise to be used as a benchmark of what an ideal trading result can be.

The trading performance results show that although in certain years, like 2000, 2002, 2005, 2007, 2010, Buy and Hold is the best strategy to behold as advocated by Fama (1965); the cumulative returns for all the 15 years from 2000 to 2014 show that Opt50MA (cumulative return of 393%) and AMA′ (cumulative return of 523%) outperform the passive

[1] The commission per contract per one way at interactive brokers for CLOF is USD0.85 while the exchange and regulatory fees in NYMEX where FCLO is traded are USD1.45.

Table 4.1 Test results on CLOF after transaction costs from 2 January 2000 to 31 December 2014

	Buy and hold (%)	*MA20 (%)*	*MAC3,21 (%)*	*MA20,0,1% (%)*	*BBZ (%)*	*Opt50MA (%)*	*AMA′ (%)*
2000	7.2	−16.9	−0.2	−9.5	1.9	−38.6	−4.5
2001	−23.5	−0.9	16.8	−2.0	7.3	−6.2	−11.1
2002	37.7	17.9	28.5	9.7	−6.7	−31.0	−5.7
2003	5.9	18.5	14.8	1.6	−1.7	18.9	−3.4
2004	37.7	−9.4	−3.3	−12.1	−18.9	−11.2	−28.3
2005	42.0	32.6	4.7	−0.9	−19.5	6.6	22.8
2006	−2.5	−13.9	−11.9	−13.7	−2.1	0.4	−25.3
2007	65.8	20.0	19.6	11.0	13.9	−9.9	22.5
2008	−46.8	42.1	−19.1	54.2	44.4	39.4	114.4
2009	46.3	−79.4	58.6	−52.1	−17.1	85.4	−48.1
2010	10.0	−17.4	−12.8	−8.9	−15.2	−8.5	0.5
2011	7.2	2.3	−16.6	−3.9	−19.5	24.8	21.2
2012	−9.0	7.4	−11.2	6.4	−4.4	13.9	6.9
2013	4.8	−12.0	−5.9	−10.8	−0.8	−2.1	2.3
2014	−42.1	4.1	14.2	8.6	3.4	−6.1	3.1
Sum of yearly returns	140.6	−5.0	76.1	−22.4	−35.1	75.7	67.3
Average return per year	9.4	−0.3	5.1	−1.5	−2.3	5.0	4.5
Cumulative return after transaction costs	127.3	47.0	24.3	66.9	−6.9	363.6	482.2
Average cumulative return per year	8.5	3.1	1.6	4.5	−0.5	24.2	32.1

Source Author's creation based on tests

threshold Buy and Hold (cumulative return of 127%). The rational investor would have earned 6.7% average return per year if he had bought and held on for 15 years from 2000 to 2014, while in the same period, the fortune teller would foretell an abnormal average return of 20% average per year while the technical analyst market practitioner earned an abnormal average of 27% after transaction costs and slippage. The net results (after taking into account transaction costs and slippage) show AMA′ outperforms all the previous trading models for the period 2000–2014. Table 4.1 shows AMA′ produces the highest profit for the in-sample period from 2 January 2000 to 31 December 2014.

Figure 4.1 shows the adaptiveness of AMA′ to CLOF prices over the last ten years. This indicates that AMA′ is a robust trading model and can be used for CLOF market. AMA′ can be taken into consideration as a viable trading model for the professional model trading desk of financial institutions. The results from this study are consistent with earlier studies like Lukac et al. (1988), Brock et al. (1992), and Balsara, Carlson, and Rao (1996), which show that simple moving averages and moving average oscillators have predictive power for the stocks in Dow Jones Industrial Average (DJIA) index.

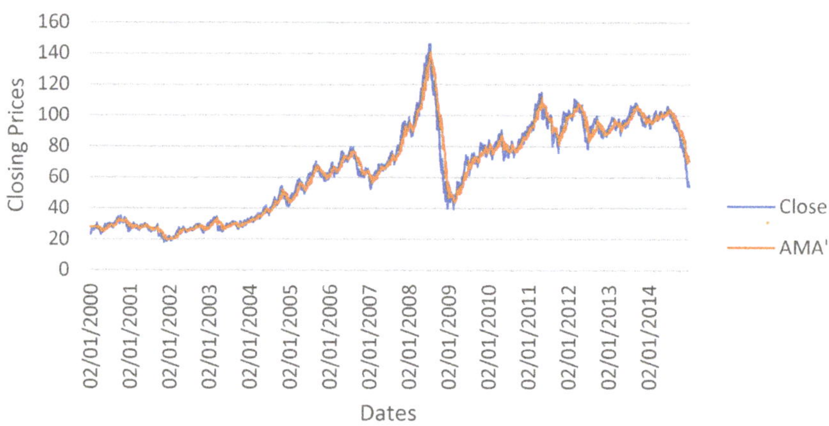

Fig. 4.1 CLOF closing prices and adjustable moving average′ (AMA′) (*Source* Author's creation based on CLOF closing prices and adjustable moving average′ [AMA′])

Conclusion: AMA′ Passes the In-Sample Profitable Tests and Needs to Be Assessed Further

From the statistical data descriptive in Chapter 3, the CLOF returns possess one of the most directional trends and seem to display excess kurtoses and time-varying volatilities. Thus, it is used to test the six technical indicators highlighted in Chapter 2. The profitability test shows that for the in-sample period from 2 January 2000 to 31 December 2014, AMA′ (cumulative return after transaction costs of 483%) outperforms the passive threshold Buy and Hold (cumulative return of 127%), MA20 (47.0%), MAC3,20 (24.3%), MAE20,1 (66.9%), BBZ (−6.9%) and even the OptMA50 (363.6%). OptMA50 is selected as the most optimal moving average after a series of tests using different lengths from 1 to 100. After this stage of in-sample test, the next stage is to verify AMA's result in the next period from 2015 to 2017 before it is put to paper test.

Review

- For the period 2000–2014 as an in-sample, the analysis has assessed the efficacy of AMA′ against 4 common technical trading rules and the threshold buy-and-hold.
- The results show that all the trading models are able to outperform the passive buy-and-hold strategy. This is consistent with the studies conducted by Lukac et al. (1988), Brock et al. (1992), and Andrada-Felix and Fernandez-Rodriguez (2008). While simple moving-average rules have outdone the other technical models ex-post, ex-ante it is extremely difficult to estimate accurately the optimal lengths to be deployed.
- Nevertheless, some researchers have also highlighted that the existence of such abnormal returns tends to diminish over time, especially so for the last decade (Olson, 2004). Hence, to outperform financial markets, increasingly sophisticated trading rules are required (Olson, 2004) due to increasing efficient market conditions in established markets (Fama, 1965). There is evidence from the literature that suggests the existence of time-varying volatility in financial and economic time-series data (Andrada-Felix & Fernandez-Rodriguez, 2008). Many have suggested that the volatility of time series in real financial markets is non-monotone and not invariant (Andrada-Felix & Fernandez-Rodriguez, 2008) and that time-varying volatility has influenced optimal portfolio configurations.

- In view of the above notions, artificial neural networks (ANN) are currently employed in finance especially in investigations of market behavior and forecasting financial time series (Atsalakis & Valavanis, 2009; Bahrammirzaee, 2010; Chan Phooi M'ng & Mehralizadeh, 2016; Gencay & Stengos, 1998).

Appendix

A trading system consists of trading rules. Most of the trading rules are very simple.

We can begin to write out the trading rules on a piece of paper, on the spreadsheet, or on a trading program. Then we either calculate the profits and losses manually or the program does it for us.

The most important aspect of a mechanical trading system is that it encompasses an automatic stop-loss exit which is predetermined at the point of entry. A mathematical algorithm is usually chosen as the proprietary trading model of the trading desk because all trading decisions are automated. With mathematical formulas, it is easier to check backtesting and optimization.

Spreadsheets are very useful in trading system modeling. They give the added advantage of visually seeing the direction of the moving average in numbers. Spreadsheets are used to eyeball the process of each trade. Eyeballing is a process of reviewing past price data in relation to the technical indicator for the purpose of making any necessary adjustments to avoid as many false trades as possible while capturing as much as the big trends as early as possible. Some confirmation conditions may also be added into the mechanical system to reduce the number of false signals. Volume and open position are good confirmation signals because they are not derived from price.

Writing the trading rules is the simple first step and writing it into charting software is easy once you know how.

Testing and simulations are all part of the practice. Analyzing the results and fine-tuning the trading system will be discussed in the next chapter.

Simple Moving Average Trading Rules

If we are using a simple moving average model, the instructions would be:

- Enter buy long: Close > Simple 20 Closes Moving Average
- Exit long sell: Close < Simple 20 Closes Moving Average
- Enter sell short: Close < Simple 20 Closes Moving Average
- Exit short buy: Close > Simple 20 Closes Moving Average

Input to the spreadsheet:

- Column A: Date
- Column B: Open
- Column C: Closing Price
- Column D: Moving Average [=average(C2:C22)]
- Column E: Buy Signal [If Column C > Column D, "**Long**", " "]
- Column F: Sell Signal [If Column C < Column D, "**Short**", " "]

On 4 January 2016, the closing price at 38.93 was less than MA at 39.27; therefore, the signal was to sell (enter short) at the open on 5 January 2016 at 39.09. The signal to buy to exit the short) at the open on 28 January 2016 at 34.99 on when the closing price on 27 January 2016 was more than MA. The profit was 4.10 and this was added to the accumulated equity (Table 4.2).

BBZ (Black Box Z-Test Statistics): BBZ Trading Rules

If we are using the BBZ model, the instructions would be:

- Enter buy long: Close > +1 × Standard Deviation from Simple 20 Closes Moving Average
- Exit long sell: Close < +1 × Standard Deviation from Simple 20 Closes Moving Average
- Enter sell short: Close < −1 × Standard Deviation from Simple 20 Closes Moving Average
- Exit short buy: Close < −1 × Standard Deviation from Simple 20 Closes Moving Average

Table 4.2 Example of how profit or loss is calculated using Close below Moving Average to enter into Short position

Date	*Open*	*Close*	*Moving average*	*Long or short*	*Entry and exit prices*	*Profit*	*Accumulated capital*
04/01/2016	39.57	38.93	39.27	Short	39.09	0	0
05/01/2016	39.09	38.23	39.02	Short	39.09	0	0
06/01/2016	38.46	36.31	38.72	Short	39.09	0	0
07/01/2016	36.45	35.64	38.49	Short	39.09	0	0
08/01/2016	35.69	35.48	38.26	Short	39.09	0	0
11/01/2016	35.18	33.69	37.97	Short	39.09	0	0
12/01/2016	33.41	32.64	37.63	Short	39.09	0	0
13/01/2016	32.94	32.35	37.33	Short	39.09	0	0
14/01/2016	32.39	33.12	37.06	Short	39.09	0	0
15/01/2016	33.17	31.38	36.67	Short	39.09	0	0
19/01/2016	31.28	30.67	36.33	Short	39.09	0	0
20/01/2016	30.76	29.69	35.96	Short	39.09	0	0
21/01/2016	30.84	31.93	35.71	Short	39.09	0	0
22/01/2016	32.22	34.67	35.60	Short	39.09	0	0
25/01/2016	34.62	33.11	35.38	Short	39.09	0	0
26/01/2016	32.7	34.22	35.14	Short	39.09	0	0
27/01/2016	33.27	35.07	34.91	Short	34.99	4.10	4.10
28/01/2016	34.99						

Source Author's creation using CLOF closing prices

Alternatively, we can calculate the Z-test statistic:

Z Close − Moving average
Standard deviation

- If (Close − Moving average) > +1 standard deviation, or Z > +1, then it is a "BUY" enter long signal.
- The "SELL" exit long signal will be when Z < +1.

And:

- If (Close − Moving average) < −1 standard deviation, or Z < −1, then it is a "SELL" enter short signal.
- The "BUY" exit short signal will be when Z > −1.

Input to the spreadsheet:

- Column A: Date
- Column B: Open
- Column C: Close
- Column D: Moving Average [=average(C2:C22)]
- Column E: Standard Deviation [=stdev(C2:C22)]
- Column F: Upper Band [=D22 + E22]
- Column G: Lower Band [=D22 − E22]
- Column H: Buy Signal [If Column C > F, "**Long**", " "]
- Column I: Sell Signal [If Column C < G, "**Short**", " "]

The calculation of the upper and lower band to determine a long or short position is shown in Table 4.3.

When the closing price on 5 January 2016 at 38.23 was less than the −1 standard deviation lower band at 38.44, the sell signal to enter short at the open on 6 January 2016 at 38.46.

The buy signal was indicated when the closing price on 22 January 2016 at 34.67 more than the −1 standard deviation lower band at 34.07, the short position was closed at the open on 25 January 2016 at 34.62. The profit is 3.84.

Table 4.3 Example of how profit or loss is calculated using Close below Lower Band to enter into Short position

Date	*Open*	*Closing prices*	*Moving average*	*Standard deviation*	*Upper band*	*Lower band*	*Long or short*	*Entry and exit prices*	*Profit*	*Accumulated equity*
05/01/2016	39.09	38.23	39.02	0.58	39.60	38.44	Short	38.46	0	0
06/01/2016	38.46	36.31	38.72	1.11	39.84	37.61	Short	38.46	0	0
07/01/2016	36.45	35.64	38.49	1.42	39.90	37.07	Short	38.46	0	0
08/01/2016	35.69	35.48	38.26	1.67	39.93	36.59	Short	38.46	0	0
11/01/2016	35.18	33.69	37.97	1.99	39.95	35.98	Short	38.46	0	0
12/01/2016	33.41	32.64	37.63	2.39	40.01	35.24	Short	38.46	0	0
13/01/2016	32.94	32.35	37.33	2.43	39.76	34.90	Short	38.46	0	0
14/01/2016	32.39	33.12	37.06	2.06	39.13	35.00	Short	38.46	0	0
15/01/2016	33.17	31.38	36.67	1.78	38.46	34.89	Short	38.46	0	0
19/01/2016	31.28	30.67	36.33	1.78	38.10	34.55	Short	38.46	0	0
20/01/2016	30.76	29.69	35.96	1.82	37.77	34.14	Short	38.46	0	0
21/01/2016	30.84	31.93	35.71	1.31	37.02	34.39	Short	38.46	0	0
22/01/2016	32.22	34.67	35.60	1.53	37.13	34.07		34.62	3.84	3.84
25/01/2016	34.62	33.11	35.38	1.56	36.94	33.81	Short	0	0	3.84

Source Author's creation using CLOF closing prices

AMA′ (Adjustable Moving Average′)

If we are using an AMA′ model, the trading decision would be:

- Enter buy long: Close > Efficacy Ratio (X) Moving Average
- Exit long sell: Close < Efficacy Ratio (X) Moving Average
- Enter sell short: Close < Efficacy Ratio (X) Moving Average
- Exit short buy: Close > Efficacy Ratio (X) Moving Average

where Efficacy Ratio (X) is the long-term standard deviation divided by the short-term standard deviation.

The inputs into the spreadsheet:

- Column A: Date
- Column B: Open
- Column C: Closing Price
- Column D: Adjustable Moving Average′ [=average(C2:C22)]
- Column E: Buy Signal [If Column C > Column D, "**Long**", " "]
- Column F: Sell Signal [If Column C < Column D, "**Short**", " "]

When the closing price on 4 January 2016 at 38.93 was less than AMA′ at 43.23, the signal was to sell short at the open on 5 January 2016 at 39.09. The buy to exit short came when the closing price on 27 January 2016 was more than AMA′. The short position was closed at the open on 28 January 2016 at 34.99. The gain was $4.10. This adds to the accumulated equity (Table 4.4).

Table 4.4 Example of how profit or loss is calculated using Close below AMA' to enter into Short position

Date	*Open*	*Closing prices*	*AMA'*	*Long or short*	*Entry and exit prices*	*Profit*	*Accumulated capital*
04/01/2016	39.57	38.93	43.23	Short	39.09	0	0
05/01/2016	39.09	38.23	43.06	Short	39.09	0	0
06/01/2016	38.46	36.31	40.62	Short	39.09	0	0
07/01/2016	36.45	35.64	39.10	Short	39.09	0	0
08/01/2016	35.69	35.48	38.62	Short	39.09	0	0
11/01/2016	35.18	33.69	37.84	Short	39.09	0	0
12/01/2016	33.41	32.64	37.40	Short	39.09	0	0
13/01/2016	32.94	32.35	37.14	Short	39.09	0	0
14/01/2016	32.39	33.12	37.52	Short	39.09	0	0
15/01/2016	33.17	31.38	37.18	Short	39.09	0	0
19/01/2016	31.28	30.67	36.94	Short	39.09	0	0
20/01/2016	30.76	29.69	37.11	Short	39.09	0	0
21/01/2016	30.84	31.93	37.85	Short	39.09	0	0
22/01/2016	32.22	34.67	36.13	Short	39.09	0	0
25/01/2016	34.62	33.11	35.78	Short	39.09	0	0
26/01/2016	32.7	34.22	35.43	Short	39.09	0	0
27/01/2016	33.27	35.07	34.91	Short	34.99	4.10	4.10
28/01/2016	34.99						

Source Author's creation using CLOF closing prices

References

Andrada-Felix, J., & Fernandez-Rodriguez, F. (2008). Improving moving average trading rules with boosting and statistical learning methods. *Journal of Forecasting, 27,* 433–449.

Atsalakis, G. S., & Valavanis, K. P. (2009). Surveying stock market forecasting techniques—Part II: Soft computing methods. *Expert Systems with Applications, 36*(3), 5932–5941.

Azizan, N. A., Mohamed, I., & Chan Phooi M'ng, J. (2011a). Profitability of technical analysis indicators: A study of an adjustable technical indicator, ABZ′, on the Malaysian futures markets. *The Business Review, 7*(2), 286–290.

Azizan, N. A., Mohamed, I., & Chan Phooi M'ng, J. (2011b). A profitability study on the Malaysian futures markets using a new adjustable technical analysis indicator, ABZ. *African Journal of Business Management, 5,* 5984–5993.

Bahrammirzaee, A. (2010). A comparative survey of artificial intelligence applications in finance: Artificial neural networks, expert system and hybrid intelligent systems. *Neural Computing and Applications, 19*(8), 1165–1195.

Balsara, N., Carlson, K., & Rao, N. (1996). Unsystematic futures profits with technical trading rules: A case for flexibility. *Journal of Financial Strategic and Decisions, 9,* 57–66.

Bessembinder, H., & Chan, K. (1998). Market efficiency and the returns to technical analysis. *Financial Management, 27*(2), 5–17.

Brock, W., Lakonishok, J., & LeBaron, B. (1992, December). Simple technical trading rules and the stochastic properties of stock returns. *Journal of Finance, 47,* 1731–1764.

Chan Phooi M'ng, J. (2018). Dynamically Adjustable Moving Average (AMA′) technical analysis indicator to forecast Asian Tigers' futures markets. *Physica A: Statistical Mechanics and Its Applications, 509,* 336–345.

Chan Phooi M'ng, J., & Mehralizadeh, M. (2016). Forecasting East Asian indices futures via a novel hybrid of wavelet-PCA denoising and artificial neural network models. *PLOS One, 11*(6), e0156338.

Fama, E. (1965). Random walks in stock market prices. *Financial Analyst Journal, 16,* 1–16.

Gandolfi, G., Rossolini, M., Sabatini, A., & Caselli, S. (2008). Dynamic MACD standard deviation embedded in MACD indicator for accurate adjustment to financial market dynamics. *IFTA Journal,* 16–23.

Gencay, R., & Stengos, T. (1998). Moving average rules, volume and the predictability of security returns with feedforward networks. *Journal of Forecasting, 17,* 401–414.

Kwon, K. Y., & Kish, R. (2002). A comparative study of technical trading strategies and return predictability: An extension of Brock, Lakonishok, and LeBaron (1992) using NYSE and NASDAQ indices. *Quarterly Review of Economics and Finance, 42,* 611–631.

Lo, A., Mamaysky, H., & Wang, J. (2000). Foundations of technical analysis: Computational algorithms, statistical inference and empirical implementation. *Journal of Finance, 55,* 1705–1765.
Lukac, L., Brorsen, B., & Irwin, S. (1988). Similarity of computer guided technical trading systems. *Journal of Futures Markets, 8*(1–13), 64.
Olson, D. (2004). Have trading rule profits in the currency markets declined over time? *Journal of Banking & Finance, 28,* 85–105.

CHAPTER 5

Development of Artificial Intelligence Algorithm Trading Systems

Abstract With easier fund management due to computational trading algorithms, which can learn from multiple sources of information, technical trading rules evolved to include artificial intelligence machine learning method using variants of neural networks. Backpropagation neural network outperforms common technical analysis indicators and traditional statistical models. Neural networks are used in machine learning by inputting past historical price data and technical indicators to predict the next output. The training is performed to achieve the lowest mean error between the predicted output and the target which is the actual close. This chapter applies a neural network enhanced technical indicator (N-CAMA′) to crude light oil futures (CLOF) which experienced high volatility in recent years.

Keywords Artificial intelligence algorithmic trading system · Artificial neural network (ANN) · Neural network enhanced technical indicator · Predicted output

Introduction

Algorithmic trading is central to the importance of trading in financial markets in recent years due to more rapid reactions to temporary mispricings and easier fund management with computational trading algorithms,

J. Chan, *Automation of Trading Machine for Traders*,
https://doi.org/10.1007/978-981-13-9945-9_5

which can learn from multiple sources of information (Atsalakis & Valavanis, 2009; Bahrammirzaee, 2010). The rapidly changing market requires more dynamic technical indicators to capture better market prediction and performance (Olson, 2004). Algorithm trading rules and technical analysis have also grown at the same time to include machine learning methods, like the artificial neural network (ANN) (Chan Phooi M'ng & Mehralizadeh, 2016).

Neural networks can be used as machine learning system by inputting past historical price data and technical indicators to predict the next output. It can train itself by making the comparison between the predicted output and the actual data of the time series which is destined the target. This process will be continuously performed to achieve the lowest mean error between the predicted output and the target (Bahrammirzaee, 2010).

The most commonly used neural network model for financial forecasting, the backpropagation neural network (Yao, Chew, & Poh, 1999) outperforms common technical analysis indicators and traditional statistical methods and models (Fernández-Pérez et al., 2012).

Technical trading techniques are still lacking in accounting for varying volatility clustering found in most financial time-series data. In light of this critical deficiency, this chapter introduces a neural network enhanced adjustable moving average (N-CAMA′) to decipher the varying trends in the market. N-CAMA′ is used to determine the weights of current close price and adjustable moving average AMA′ (Chan Phooi M'ng, 2018).

Extending the research of Yao et al. (1999) that employs neural network to combine the different technical indicators, this study investigates the viability of this method fast forward to current period. Different from Yao et al. (1999), this study employs AMA′ alongside with the current close price to predict the next period's close. Comparing this predicted future close, against the current close, the approach similar to Yao et al. (1999) is to buy at the next day's open when the predicted close is higher than the current close. This approach is chosen based on recent findings that methods using ANNs to combine the technical indicators have produced better out-of-sample results than most of the single and fixed moving average rules (Andrada-Felix & Fernandez-Rodriguez, 2008).

Heeding on this notion, this chapter applies a neural network enhanced technical analysis in the context of crude light oil futures (CLOF). The main rationale of applying the analysis on the oil market is due to the high volatility in its prices observed in recent years. Understanding the nature of the stochastic behavior of oil fluctuations is of crucial importance for policy and decision makers, not only at national-level economies but also in financial markets (Cevik & Sedik, 2011). In view of these factors, this study proposes an innovated AMA′ technical indicator model using neural network to investigate the behavior of CLOF prices traded in Chicago Mercantile Exchange (CME); in an attempt to decipher trends in these financial markets.

The objectives here are twofold. First, it aims to predict the future prices of CLOF, using the neural network enhanced Close and AMA′ (N-CAMA′); and second, to determine if the abnormal returns derived from using those predicted values are significant. This study evaluates the efficacy of N-CAMA′ to generate abnormal returns and to provide evidence of the existence of market anomalies that would support the notion on the feasibility of gaining excess returns above the threshold buy-and-hold in the long run. This chapter also assesses the N-CAMA′ against the moving averages, BBZ (Chan, 2005, 2006) as well as AMA′.

In this study, we propose a simple forecasting approach, which inputs the close and adjustable moving average into the nonlinear autoregressive ANN (NARNNX) in the preprocessing stage to develop an ensemble forecasting model, N-CAMA′ to predict the next period's close. This output will be used in the modeling stage to generate automated buy or sell signals. The results of the prediction accuracy shown in hit rate and the profitability performance will be evaluated.

Architecture of Artificial Intelligence Trading System

Nonlinear Autoregressive Neural Network with Exogenous Inputs (NARNNX)

ANNs are sets of simple interconnected factors processing information used for pattern recognition. Each connection of the neural network gets a weight attached to it. ANN is used to combine the technical indicators to produce better out-of-sample result than single and fixed moving average rules (Andrada-Felix & Fernandez-Rodriguez, 2008).

Heeding on this notion, this chapter applies a neural network enhanced technical analysis in the context of CLOF. The main rationale of applying the analysis on the oil market is due to the high volatility in its prices observed in recent years.

The feedforward backpropagation neural network (FBNN) algorithm appears as one of the most broadly used machine learning techniques for multilayer networks. The standard feedforward backpropagation neural network generally contains an input layer, several hidden layers, and an output layer. The elements in the network are linked in a feedforward style. The weights of the links have been set as initial values. The error term between the actual value and the predicted output value is backpropagated across the network for the weights to be revised in order to minimize the error between the predicted and the actual value.

Nonlinear autoregressive neural network with exogenous inputs (NARNNX) is a kind of recurrent dynamic neural network with feedback links connecting some layers of the network. We chose NARNNX because Siegelmann, Horne, and Giles (1997) show that NARNNX networks perform better on problems involving long-term dependencies. As opposed to other recurrent networks, NARNNX has a limited feedback which comes only from the output neuron rather than from hidden states (Siegelmann et al., 1997). However, using such an approach there is no bound to the number of nodes required to achieve a good approximation. Furthermore, it is not clear how such systems relate to conventional models of computational intelligence. The NARNNX model is built on the linear autoregressive exogenous (ARX) method, which is generally applied in time series modeling.

The fundamental equation for the NARNNX model is:

$$y(t) = f(y(t-1), y(t-2), \ldots, y(t-d), x(t-1), x(t-2), \ldots, x(t-d)) \tag{5.1}$$

where the obtained value of the dependent output signal $y(t)$ is regressed on d former values of the target signal $y(t)$ and d previous values of exogenous (independent) input signals $x(t)$. One can implement the NARNNX model by applying a feedforward and backpropagation neural network (FBNN) to estimate the function f. Moreover, weights and biases in an FBNN will be adjusted continuously to minimize the error term between output ($y^*(t+1)$) and target value ($y(t+1)$) to achieve the lowest mean of the error terms. The backpropagation neural network employs a training process of error backpropagation which uses recursive gradient descent method that minimizes the sum of squared errors of the system by moving down the gradient error curve (Fernandez-Rodrıguez et al., 2000). Error backpropagation makes it possible to approximate nonlinear functions. The training continues until generalization stops improving by an increase in normalized mean square error of the validation sample. The values of the weights are determined by an iterative learning process and their transformation at each successive layer is determined by a specific transfer function.

N-CAMA′ (One Hidden Layer, Ten Neutrons, 2 Delays ANN Model Using Closing Prices and AMA′)

In this experiment, the close and AMA′ are processed as inputs. Using 10 neurons, 2 delays, 1 hidden layer, and Levenberg-Marquardt optimization, 2000–2014 data is used for training. The output is then used as the predicted close for the next day.

The technical trading rules used are the same commonly used ones in Lukac, Brorsen, and Irwin (1988) and Brock, Lakonishok, and LeBaron (1992), for comparison purpose. The purpose of the moving averages tests used by Lukac et al. (1988) and Brock et al. (1992) is to ascertain whether the application of moving average trading rules is able to generate higher returns compared to the passive buy-and-hold strategy and, in particular, whether the neural network enhanced Close Adjustable Moving Average Prime (N-CAMA′) is able to outperform the most optimized moving average commonly used by Lukac et al. (1988), Brock et al. (1992), and the market practitioners. The training period is from 2 January 2000 to 31 December 2014 while the validation period is from 2 January 2015 to 31 December 2017 and the out-of-sample period is from 2 January 2018 to 31 December 2018. The method used here in this study is similar to the approach used by Yao et al. (1999) which is to long the futures when the predicted output is higher than the current close and to short otherwise.

The objective of this exercise is to determine whether the abnormal return from utilizing the forecast of next period's price is significantly higher than the passive buy-and-hold control. If $\hat{c}_{t+1} > C_t$, where, $\hat{c}_{t+1}$ is the predicted closing price output for the next period, and C_t is the current closing price, the trading strategy is to buy, and if otherwise, the strategy is to sell. The procedure is first, to compute the adjustable moving averages prime (AMA′) for CLOF from 2000 to 2014; then using inputs of close prices and AMA′, NARNNX generates predicted output; finally using the resultant predicted output, profit or loss is computed from the trading signals.

In this simulation, after AMA′ values are computed, the close prices and these AMA′ values are fed into a one-layer, 10 neurons, two-period delay configuration NARNNX. The predicted outputs are used in the trading strategy to determine the trading signal by comparing the predicted output for the next period with the actual current closing price. If the predicted output for the next period is higher than the current closing price, the signal will be processed as a *buy long*, otherwise, the signal will be a sell short. If $\hat{c}_{t+1} > C_t$, where, $\hat{c}_{t+1}$ is the predicted close price output for the next period, and C_t is the current close price, then the trading strategy is to buy, otherwise, the course of action is to sell.

According to Yao et al. (1999), a prediction that closely follows the trend of the actual target would result in a low minimized squared error (NMSE).

We ran tests from one to 15 neurons. Interestingly, 10-neurons ANN model is selected in accordance with the earlier tests to employ the model with the least NMSE.

Artificial Intelligence System N-CAMA's Abnormal Returns

In this section, performances of the neural network close AMA′ (N-CAMA′) trading model are evaluated against all the selected trading models. The summed return of this trading rule can be calculated by the following equation and used as a comparison scale among the models and markets:

$$\text{Return}(\%) = 100 \times \left(\sum_{t=1}^{b} \left(\frac{y_{t+1} - y_t}{y_t} \right) + \sum_{t=1}^{s} \left(\frac{y_t - y_{t+1}}{y_t} \right) \right) \tag{5.2}$$

where b denotes the total number of long positions and s represents the total number of short positions.

The base price of \$23.87.00 for CLOF as at the opening of 2 January 2000 is used. The net percentage cumulative returns after transaction costs and 1 tick slippage are computed by taking the gains/losses as percentages of the base price. Table 5.1 depicts the net percentage returns after transaction costs. The trading performance results show that although in certain years, like 2000, 2002, 2005, 2007, 2010, Buy and Hold is the best strategy

Table 5.1 Trading results of N-CAMA′ against buy and hold, MA20, MA3,21, MA20,01%, BBZ, the most optimized Opt50 and AMA′

	Buy and hold (%)	*MA20 (%)*	*MAC3,21 (%)*	*MA20,0,1 (%)*	*BBZ (%)*	*Opt50MA (%)*	*AMA′ (%)*	*N-CAMA′ (%)*
2000	7.2	−16.9	−0.2	−9.5	1.9	−38.6	−4.5	−8.3
2001	−23.5	−0.9	16.8	−2.0	7.3	−6.2	−11.1	−15.4
2002	37.7	17.9	28.5	9.7	−6.7	−31.0	−5.7	−23.7
2003	5.9	18.5	14.8	1.6	−1.7	18.9	−3.4	43.2
2004	37.7	−9.4	−3.3	−12.1	−18.9	−11.2	−28.3	55.3
2005	42.0	32.6	4.7	−0.9	−19.5	6.6	22.8	4.1
2006	−2.5	−13.9	−11.9	−13.7	−2.1	0.4	−25.3	−0.4
2007	65.8	20.0	19.6	11.0	13.9	−9.9	22.5	49.5
2008	−46.8	42.1	−19.1	54.2	44.4	39.4%	114.4	39.8
2009	46.3	−79.4	58.6	−52.1	−17.1	85.4	−48.1	−37.3
2010	10.0	−17.4	−12.8	−8.9	−15.2	−8.5	0.5	−2.4
2011	7.2	2.3	−16.6	−3.9	−19.5	24.8	21.2	24.6
2012	−9.0	7.4	−11.2	6.4	−4.4	13.9	6.9	25.2
2013	4.8	−12.0	−5.9	−10.8	−0.8	−2.1	2.3	−5.0
2014	−42.1	4.1	14.2	8.6	3.4	−6.1	3.1	2.3
Sum of Yearly Returns	140.6	−5.0	76.1	−22.4	−35.1	75.7	67.3	151.6
Average return per year	9.4	−0.3	5.1	−1.5	−2.3	5.0	4.5	10.1
Cumulative Return after transaction costs	127.3	47.0	24.3%	66.9	−6.9	363.6	482.2	499.2
Average Cumulative Return per year	8.5	3.1	1.6	4.5	−0.5	24.2	32.1	33.3

Source Author's creation based on tests

to behold as advocated by Fama, 1965; the cumulative returns after transaction costs for all the 15 years from 2000 to 2014 show that Opt50MA (cumulative return of 363%), AMA′ (cumulative return of 482%) and N-CAMA′ (cumulative return of 499%) outperform the passive threshold Buy and Hold (cumulative return of 127%). The rational investor would have earned 6.7% average return per year if he had bought and held on for 15 years from 2000 to 2014, while in the same period, the fortune teller would foretell an abnormal average return of 24% average per year; the technical analyst market practitioner earned an abnormal average of 32%, and the black box neural adjustable trader earned an more acceptable abnormal return of 33% after transaction costs and slippage. The net results (after taking into account transaction costs and slippage) show N-CAMA′ outperforms all the previous trading models (Fig. 5.1).

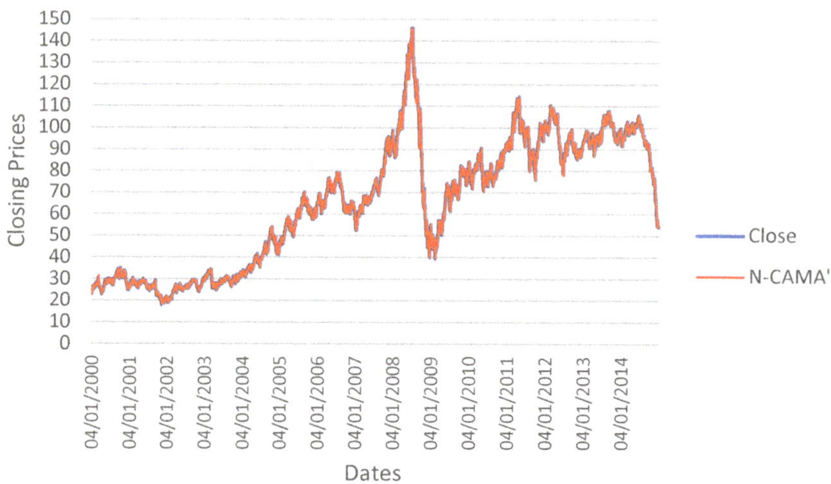

Fig. 5.1 CLOF closing prices and Neural network of Close and AMA′ (N-CAMA′) (*Source* Author's creation based on CLOF closing prices and neural network of close and AMA′ [N-CAMA′])

Conclusion

N-CAMA′ surpasses all the models tests and should be further assessed for viability.

The initial trading performance results indicate that N-CAMA′ is a robust trading model and can be used for CLOF market. N-CAMA′ can be taken into consideration as a viable trading model for the professional model trading desk of financial institutions.

We compare N-CAMA′ along with the other common technical trading models (MA, MAC, MA 1% Envelope Bands) and the passive buy-and-hold strategy. For the period 2000–2014 as a sample, the analysis has assessed the efficacy of N-CAMA′ against the other common technical trading rules and the threshold buy-and-hold and found that it can outperform all of them with a superior return of 500% or a statistically significant profit of 33.3% per annum.

N-CAMA′ is new technical indicator that can contribute to the profits of the model trading desk. The ability of N-CAMA′ to predict indicates a new direction for research in incremental machine learning trading systems.

Before N-CAMA′ can be applied for trading in professional model trading desk, there are some more tests and evaluations to be done and this is discussed in the next few chapters. Testing and simulations are all part of the practice. Analyzing the results and fine-tuning the trading system will be discussed in the next chapter.

With NARNNX and any other neural network, the main drawback as Kaastra and Boyd (1996) have noted is the large number of combinations of inputs, neurons, hidden layers, and delays; deciding on the appropriate network paradigm still involves much trial and error. Having said that, with good preliminary results, future research can explore and find better fit for this and other world commodities futures.

Review

- Algorithmic trading is central to the importance of trading in financial markets in recent years due to easier and faster computational trading program. Algorithm trading rules and technical analysis have also grown at the same time to include machine learning methods, like the ANN. Neural networks can be used as machine learning system by inputting past historical price data and technical indicators to predict the next output. It can train itself by making the comparison between the predicted output and the actual data of the time series which is destined the target. This process will be continuously performed to achieve the lowest mean error between the predicted output and the target. The most commonly used neural network model for financial forecasting, the backpropagation neural network outperforms common technical analysis indicators and traditional statistical methods and models.

- Neural network enhanced adjustable moving average (N-CAMA′) determines the weights of current close price and adjustable moving average AMA′ to decipher the varying trends in the market. Comparing this predicted future close, against the current close, the approach adopted by this trading system is to buy at the next day's open when the predicted close is higher than the current close.
- The cumulative returns after transaction costs for all the 15 years from 2000 to 2014 show that Opt50MA (cumulative return of 363%), AMA′ (cumulative return of 482%) and N-CAMA′ (cumulative return of 499%) outperform the passive threshold Buy and Hold (cumulative return of 127%). The rational investor would have earned 6.7% average return per year if he had bought and held on for 15 years from 2000 to 2014, while in the same period, the fortune teller would foretell an abnormal average return of 24% average per year; the technical analyst market practitioner earned an abnormal average of 32%, and the black box neural adjustable trader earned an more acceptable abnormal return of 33% after transaction costs and slippage. The net results (after taking into account transaction costs and slippage) show N-CAMA′ outperforms all the previous trading models.

Appendix

In this study, MATLAB's "narxnet" NARNNX is used to establish a one-step-ahead prediction model. The NARNNX model is built on the linear ARX method, which is generally applied in time series modeling.

The fundamental equation for the NARX model is:

$$\hat{c}_{t+1} = f\left(C_t, C_{t-1}, \ldots, C_{t-d}, \mathrm{AMA}_t, \mathrm{AMA}_{t-1}, \ldots, \mathrm{AMA}_{t-d}\right) \tag{5.3}$$

where the obtained value of the dependent output signal $\hat{c}_{t+1}$ is regressed on d former values of the target signal C_t and d previous values of exogenous (independent) input signals AMA_t. NARNNX model by applying a FBNN to estimate the function f. Moreover, weights and biases in an FBNN will be adjusted continuously to minimize the error term between output $\hat{c}_{t+1}$ and target C_t to achieve the lowest mean of the error terms.

The architecture of a NARX network includes the number of hidden layers, the number of delays (the number of past data of that network that account for training), and portions of training, validation, and testing. NARX networks divide the data into three subsets: training set, validation set, and testing set, which sets will be spread randomly along the time series, with a configured percentage for each of them; in this study, the proportions are training 75%, validation 15%, and testing 15%.

In this experiment, the close and AMA′ are processed as inputs. Using 10 neurons, 2 delays, 1 hidden layer, and Levenberg-Marquardt optimization, 2000–2014 data is used for training. The output is then used as the predicted close for the next day.

The training period is from 2 January 2000 to 31 December 2014 while the validation period is from 2 January 2015 to 31 December 2017 and the out-of-sample period is from 2 January 2018 to 31 December 2018. The method used is similar to the approach used by Yao et al. (1999) which is to long the futures when the predicted output is higher than the current close and to short otherwise.

We ran tests from one to 15 neurons. Interestingly, 10-neurons ANN model is selected in accordance with the earlier tests to employ the model with the least NMSE.

Although the best architecture to apply depends on the type of the problem to be solved by the network, there is no rule of thumb to select the number of hidden layers and delays (Kaastra & Boyd, 1996). In this study, Levenberg-Marquardt optimization is used as the training algorithm, which is a built-in.

The objective of this exercise is to determine whether the abnormal return from utilizing the forecast of next period's price is significantly higher than the passive buy-and-hold control. If $\hat{c}_{t+1} > C_t$, where, $\hat{c}_{t+1}$ is the predicted closing price output for the next period, and C_t is the current closing price, the trading strategy is to buy, and if otherwise, the strategy is to sell.

The results of the prediction accuracy shown in hit rate and the profitability performance will be evaluated.

References

Andrada-Felix, J., & Fernandex-Rodriguez, F. (2008). Improving moving average trading rules with boosting and statistical learning methods. *Journal of Forecasting, 27*, 433–449.

Atsalakis, G. S., & Valavanis, K. P. (2009). Surveying stock market forecasting techniques—Part II: Soft computing methods. *Expert Systems with Applications, 36*(3), 5932–5941.

Bahrammirzaee, A. (2010). A comparative survey of artificial intelligence applications in finance: Artificial neural networks, expert system and hybrid intelligent systems. *Neural Computing and Applications, 19*(8), 1165–1195.

Brock, W., Lakonishok, J., & LeBaron, B. (1992, December). Simple technical trading rules and the stochastic properties of stock returns. *Journal of Finance, 47*(5), 1731–1764.

Cevik, S., & Sedik, T. (2011). *A barrel of oil or a bottle of wine: How do global growth dynamics affect commodity prices?* (Working Paper 11/01). Washington, DC: International Monetary Fund.

Chan, J. (2005, March/April). Using time series volatilities to trade trends: Trading technique—BBZ. *Australian Technical Analysts Association Journal*, 31–38.

Chan, J. (2006, March). Trading trends with the Bollinger bands Z-Test. *Technical Analysis of Stocks & Commodities, 24*(3), 46–52.

Chan Phooi M'ng, J., & Mehralizadeh, M. (2016). Forecasting East Asian indices futures via a novel hybrid of wavelet-PCA denoising and artificial neural network models. *PLOS One, 11*(6), e0156338.

Chan Phooi M'ng, J. (2018). Dynamically adjustable moving average (AMA') technical analysis indicator to forecast Asian Tigers' futures markets. *Physica A: Statistical Mechanics and Its Applications, 509*, 336–345.

Fernández-Pérez, A., Fernández-Rodríguez, F., & Sosvilla-Rivero, S. (2012). Detecting trends in the foreign exchange markets. *Applied Economics Letters, 19*(5), 493–503.

Fernandez-Rodnguez, F., Gonzalez-Martel, C., & Sosvilla-Rivero, S. (2000). On the profitability of technical trading rules based on artificial neural networks: Evidence from the Madrid stock market. *Economic Letters, 69*(1), 89–94.

Kaastra, I., & Boyd, M. (1996). Designing a neural network for forecasting financial and economic time series. *Neurocomputing, 10*(3), 215–236.

Lukac, L., Brorsen, B., & Irwin, S. (1988). Similarity of computer guided technical trading systems. *Journal of Futures Markets, 8*, 1–13, 64.

Olson, D. (2004). Have trading rule profits in the currency markets declined over time? *Journal of Banking & Finance, 28*, 85–105.

Siegelmann, H. T., Horne, B. G., & Giles, C. L. (1997). Computational capabilities of recurrent NARX neural networks. *IEEE Transactions on Systems, Man, and Cybernetics, Part B: Cybernetics, 27*(2), 208–215.

Yao, J., Chew, L. T., & Poh, H.-L. (1999). Neural networks for technical analysis: A study on KLCI. *International Journal of Theoretical and Applied Finance, 2*(2), 221–241.

CHAPTER 6

Test Results of the Profitability of New Trading Model

Abstract Test results of trading systems are analyzed to choose the model with the largest profit and least drawdown. After selecting the most profitable security, simulation tests for MA20, MA(3,20), MA(20,1%), BBZ, AMA′ and N-CAMA′ are conducted. From 2000 to 2014, the net profit after transaction costs for N-CAMA′ is very profitable at an average of \$7.94 per annum. The large number of profitable trades makes N-CAMA′ look attractive. However, N-CAMA's average gain is smaller (0.98) to average loss (−1.58). The maximum consecutive losses show that N-CAMA′ experienced the highest maximum consecutive losses of \$38.10 for 16 consecutive trades from 23 December 2008 to 5 March 2009. N-CAMA′, thus requires further optimization and tuning especially in cutting losses during and after the evaluation period.

Keywords Neural network enhanced Close and Adjustable Moving Average′ (N-CAMA′) · Simulation tests · Profitability · Hits · Maximum consecutive drawdowns

Introduction

Technical analysis is built on the ground that even though the past is not a true and accurate representation of the future, it is the best experience we have got. Quantitatively, we use the model that we have worked with

J. Chan, *Automation of Trading Machine for Traders*,
https://doi.org/10.1007/978-981-13-9945-9_6

for the past many years which optimized parameters worked in recent past. Based on the assumption that what had worked in the last few months will most probably work to predict the next day's direction, the next day's target is predicted. In order to get the odds in our favor, we will analyze how the trading model performed in the past ten years.

The obvious objective of having a trading system is to make life simple and trading accountable. A trading system is the only professional way to go about trading. Before you start trading any market, backtesting a trading system using historical prices will give the trader valuable information, which he can use for his projections and trading strategy.

This means that at the point of entry, the trader knows exactly what his maximum loss should be (Chan, 2011). All mechanical trading systems must be quantifiable and involve no human judgment. The trading model analysis consists of the number of hits the next period prediction was correct. Hit is counted when the next period's prediction was correct. After knowing the number of hits, the average gain must be more than average loss. Next is to analyze the loss patterns. The thing to look out for in the losses is the amount of the maximum consecutive losses. This amount is the determinant of whether the apparently profitable trading model will be successful in the long run.

This amount may also be the amount at which an automatic stop-loss exit can be determined. Based on this assumption, the current loss at any point in the time should not exit the largest loss that the trading model had experienced for the given product for the last say ten years. This stop-loss order will be placed at the point of entry and revised periodically as the trade moves in the favorable direction of the generated signal.

This section explores the analysis of test results of trading systems for the purpose of choosing the model with the combination of the highest number of hits, largest profit, and least drawdown.

Analysis of Trading Systems

After choosing your selected security, which in this case, is the crude light oil futures (CLOF), run the simulation tests in your program for the different models, MA20, MA(3,20), MA(20,1%), BBZ, AMA′ and N-CAMA′. All the trading models may be replicated in the spreadsheets.

Analyzing Test Results

View Results

Profit

First calculate and look at the largest profit per annum or per quarter. Note and observe if the parameters are consistent with previous years and quarters. Choose the parameters that most frequent produce the largest profit in recent times. After taking into account the number of trades incurred and the net profit after transaction costs, the trader is in a better position to assess if it is profitably worthwhile to trade the particular instrument. The net profit after the numerous trades and hefty transaction costs may not be able to cover possible slippage and be worth the time and effort to trade that particular instrument compared with another which yields the same kind of net profit but lesser trades and transaction costs.

Number of Hits

Hits are the number of profitable trades to total number of trades. Note and observe the number of hits. After comparing the total number of trades, it may be psychologically important for the trader to check if he can accept the percentage of winning trades to losing ones. If the percentage is too small, then those traders who enjoy the thrill of winning may abandon the trading system. A ratio of 50:50, 50% winning trades to 50% losing trades is acceptable and realistic of a binomial outcome.

Average Gain to Average Loss

Find the trading model with the largest average gain to average loss. Is this the largest profit model with the largest number of hits? If so, then you should choose this trading model. Otherwise, note and observe the losses patterns. If the ratio is 50:50, 50% winning trades to 50% losing trades, knowing the average gain to average loss is important. The average gain must not be the same as the average loss; if so, it would be a losing game after paying transaction costs to the brokers. My rule of thumb is to look for average gain to average loss of three to one, 3 times average profit to average loss or limit the loss to roughly one-third (1/3) of projected profit. This is because the trading system used is a trending system, which means that the profits earned during trending periods are more than enough to cover the whipsaw losses in range trading. Most of the time, the average gain to average loss ratio would be recorded in evaluation as two to one; 2 times average profit to average loss because of slippages, that is, the actual transacted trades are worse off than the last done price recorded for the period.

Maximum Consecutive Losses

Before you decide on the trading model with the largest profit, largest number of hits and largest average gain to average loss, check the maximum consecutive losses. Look at the maximum drawdown of the chart and trading model. Is the maximum drawdown too large relative to the gains? The most important consideration in the adoption of any trading system is the maximum consecutive losses, which is the cumulative losses that accumulated consecutively. A huge cumulative loss in relation to the net profit of comparable sizes would be undesirable. This would impact the trader negatively in terms of capital outlay as well as psychologically. It is not easy to handle losses, no matter how small they are, let alone losses after losses continuously. Therefore, it would wise to choose a trading system that has the smaller maximum consecutive loss given the same kind of net profit. In other words, the trader chooses the trading system with the smaller consecutive loss to net profit ratio.

Empirical Results and Discussion on Findings

The empirical results of the tests on the trading models for the in-sample period of 15 years from 2000 to 2014 are tabulated into the above categories for comparison and further discussion.

Using the above simulation tests (which include transaction costs), the profit results for CLOF are shown in Table 6.1. In trading models, the profitability checklist of trading system includes many items, the most important of which that the experienced trader looks for are:

1. Net profit after transaction costs
   From this return analysis, it is found that the classical technical rules are no longer as profitable as they used to be; and that the annual average cumulative returns from the 15 years after transaction costs do not warrant or justify the employment of MA20, MA3,20, MA20,1% and BBZ. However, for the period of 2000–2014, AMA′ and N-CAMA′ are very profitable at \$7.67 (32% return per annum against the base value of \$23.87 at the opening of 2 January 2000) and \$7.94 (33%

Table 6.1 Analysis of returns from tested trading models for in-sample period (2000–2014)

	MA20	*MA(3,21)*	*MA(20,1%)*	*BBZ*	*OptMA*	*AMA′*	*N-CAMA′*
Net cumulative profit after transaction costs (per year)	\$0.76	\$0.39	\$1.06	\$(0.11)	\$5.79	\$7.67	\$7.94
Number of profitable trades to unprofitable trades	128:298	89:185	136:295	129:293	66:217	115:264	1168:646
Average profit to average loss	3.48:−1.46	4.18:−1.98	2.91:−1.29	2.77:−1.22	5.16:−1.17	3.95:−1.28	0.98:−1.58
Maximum consecutive losses	−22.6 11 periods	−24.56 3 periods	−15.2 3 periods	−15.59 3 periods	−29.7 12 periods	−16.48 9 periods	−38.1 16 periods

Source Author's creation based on tests

return per annum yearly since the opening at $23.87 on 2 January 2000). This kind of in-sample average yearly return justifies further investigations on and into AMA′ and N-CAMA′ trading models for another evaluation and out-of-sample testing periods (from 2015 to current).

2. Number of profitable trades to unprofitable trades
   The number of profitable trades is very much less than unprofitable trades for all the above models except for N-CAMA′. This large number of profitable trades makes N-CAMA′ look attractive and justifies further examination.
3. Average gain to average loss
   Except for N-CAMA′, the much larger average gains for the trading models make up for smaller number of profitable trades. Most of the average gains pass the 3 (three) times more than average losses' rule of thumb. As for N-CAMA′, further testing is required as the average gain is smaller (0.98) to average loss (−1.58). N-CAMA′ is not as attractive as it first look and further optimization and tuning is required in the evaluation period.
4. Maximum consecutive losses
   The maximum consecutive losses, which is one of the most important statistics in any trading model shows that N-CAMA′ experienced the highest maximum consecutive losses of $38.10 for 16 consecutive trades from 23 December 2008 to 5 March 2009. This losses experience is not psychologically damaging for the trader, but it is a set back for his equity and trading track record. The maximum consecutive losses are considered very high compared to the average gain of $7.94 per year and against margin requirement of USD2700. (A loss of USD38,100 would result in margin call to the trader to top up his maintenance margin at least 14 times.) In this example, the $38.10 consecutive losses came after a gain of 42 for the year 2008. Thus, the trader is able to take the losses financially and psychologically. A new trader who starts with this kind of consecutive losses would have had repeated margin calls. This shows that trading requires a lot of patience and persistence. N-CAMA′ is found to be not as attractive as it first appears to be, and further optimization and tuning especially in cutting loss is required during and after the evaluation period.

After the in-sample period test to learn the behavior of the time series had been performed, an out-of-sample period test should be carefully conducted to evaluate, validate, and confirm the results of in-sample period test.

Conclusion: N-CAMA′ Needs a Stop to Proceed

N-CAMA′ is not as attractive as it initially looks like; the maximum consecutive losses totaling \$38.10 for 16 consecutive trades from 23 December 2008 to 5 March 2009 is relatively too high compared to the average gain of \$7.94 per year and against margin requirement of USD2700. The trader would have to top up his maintenance margin at least 14 times. Thus, it would be prudent to set a stop loss in the trading system. A stop loss of \$6 can be inputted into the system.

While it is the ambition of every trader to find the perfect trading system, as with any trading system there are always flaws, whether it is pattern recognition or technical indicators like moving averages. So, the ideal trading system is not a perfect system but the one that makes the most return at the lowest risk and lowest number of false entries. It is every trader's quest to find the perfect trading system. As too many trading systems are similar, it is best to design, construct, and test a totally original trading system so that others will not know your support, resistance, and especially your stop orders. This is to prevent your stops being triggered unnecessarily. Therefore, the ideal trading system is your own original, time-tested scheme.

We will work with a stop loss in the next section of capital money management.

Review

- A mechanical trading program is defined as a completely automated trading system. It can be in the form of software or it can be on a piece of paper. Having an objective mathematical trading program ensures that all trading decisions can be acted upon mechanically. All trades must be accounted for by the mechanical system when audited. Transparency is thus ensured.
- The trading rules on when to enter and exit can be written down in a trading program.

- A profit analysis table can be used for performance evaluation. A profit analysis checks for net profit after transaction costs, number of profitable trades to unprofitable trades, average profit to average loss and maximum consecutive losses to ensure that the trading capital is sufficient to last through bad times.
- For the period of 2000–2014, the net profit after transaction costs for N-CAMA′ is very profitable at an average of $7.94 (33% return per annum yearly since the opening at $23.87 on 2 January 2000). This kind of in-sample average yearly return justifies further investigations on and into N-CAMA′ trading models for another evaluation and out-of-sample testing periods (from 2015 to current).
- N_CAMA's number of profitable trades are very much more than unprofitable trades which is not the case for the other moving averages and BBZ trading models. This large number of profitable trades makes N-CAMA′ look attractive and justifies further examination.
- However, N-CAMA's average gain is smaller (0.98) to average loss (−1.58). N-CAMA′ is not as attractive as it first look and further fine-tuning like set the stop loss and inputting the stop loss into the trading system is required in the evaluation period.
- The maximum consecutive losses show that N-CAMA′ experienced the highest maximum consecutive losses of $38.10 for 16 consecutive trades from 23 December 2008 to 5 March 2009 is extremely high compared to the average gain of $7.94 per year and against margin requirement of USD2700. N-CAMA′ is found to be not as attractive as it first appears to be, and further optimization and tuning especially in cutting loss is required during and after the evaluation period.
- After the in-sample period test to learn the behavior of the time series had been performed, an out-of-sample period test should be carefully conducted to evaluate, validate, and confirm the results of in-sample period test.

Reference

Chan, J. (2011). *Financial Times guide to technical analysis: How to trade like a professional.* London, UK: Financial Times Prentice-Hall.

CHAPTER 7

Evaluation and Stops

Abstract The trading models must be periodically evaluated to trace common patterns in the profits and losses to look for methods to avoid unnecessary losing trades and to improve the timing of the winning trades. This will assess the fitness of the assigned parameters to the current market condition. The objective of the out-of-sample test is to confirm the trading instrument with the chosen strategy is the best choice. Another equally important consideration, money management is risk management with adequate capital. The most professional way to execute stop loss is to place stop order at the entry of a new position. If a stop loss of $6 had been used for N-CAMA′, the profits would have been 150 for in-sample period and 447 for evaluation period.

Keywords Periodic profit/loss evaluation · Money and capital management · Out-of-sample test · Stop loss

Introduction

Anyone will know if his trading strategy is not working well for his capital will dwindle. Some traders will not admit it until it is too late, that is when all their capital had depleted. Some change too fast and find that right after they changed the trading model, the trend they had envisaged materialized and he is faced with what is commonly known as trader's remorse.

J. Chan, *Automation of Trading Machine for Traders*,
https://doi.org/10.1007/978-981-13-9945-9_7

If your strategy is working, then you just do more of it. If it is not, then you will have to re-evaluate your trading strategy from the first step. If all is in order, then you should decide if your capital can last through this bad time for you to profit from the "big one" as I call it (Chan, 2011).

Trading is about lasting through bad times. If your capital can last through the first series of bad times, it will definitely grow during the good times. This section talks about how to lose; how to stop loss early and how to place stop-loss order. It talks of the right order.

The results of the out-of-sample test from 2015 to 2017 are discussed to examine the objectives.

- If the trading strategy you have chosen the best for the series that you have chosen; and
- If the series that you have chosen the best/most profitable one in the period.

This section begins with evaluating the validation of the out-of-sample test.

Evaluation

Evaluation can be done at any time, and quarterly and annual evaluations are common practice. The trading record can be compiled from the monthly or quarterly reports of all your transactions. If your trading decisions were automated, then it would be an analysis of results. Otherwise, a trading journal of your trading system generated signals, and the execution can be used for evaluation purpose. This trading journal will enable periodic postmortem evaluation of trades, comparison of realized, and unrealized losses and gains (whether it is due to slippage or indiscipline), and provide the trader a road map on how to improve on his trading; at the chosen trading model, trading strategy or capital management. The ultimate purpose of the periodic evaluation is to trace common patterns in the profits and losses and to evaluate the actual realized return against the projected profit and the actual realized losses against the permissible risk. The idea is to look for methods to avoid unnecessary losing trades and to improve the timing of the winning trades. This will assess the parameters that are most fitting to the current phase.

We can begin comparing the in-sample returns where the trading models learn the behavior of the time series, CLOF, and the returns in the evaluation period.

Table 7.1 shows that in accordance with Random Walk hypothesis (Fama, 1965); Buy and Hold produces the highest return in 2016 and 2017; however, Evaluation of the performance of the N-CAMA′ shows that it outperforms Buy and Hold in sum of yearly returns (82 vs 47%), average return per year (27 vs 15%), cumulative return after transaction costs (144 vs 23%), and average cumulative return per year (448.3 vs 7.9%). N-CAMA′ also outperforms its peers by the sum of returns with average return of 27.51% per annum for the 3 years in evaluation.

However, upon closer analysis, in these 3 years, according to cumulative return after transaction costs, MA (3,21,0%) and BBZ (Chan, 2005, 2006) outperform N-CAMA′ with average cumulative return of 48.9 and 52.9% per year against N-CAMA's average of 48.3%. This shows that the market is dynamic in nature, and its natural characteristics keep evolving such that different trading models cater better to different market periods.

Comparing the market in the two periods (2000–2014) and (2015–2017) shows that the average cumulative return is about 8%, while N-CAMA′ gives an average cumulative return of 36% for the whole period (33% for 2000–2014 period and 48% for 2015–2017 period).

Upon closer periodic analysis from Table 7.2, it confirms that different trading models work better in different periods. MA20 performs badly with average cumulative return of 3.1% in the in-sample period while doing better with 33.1% average annual return in the evaluation period. In either period, the Buy and Hold (average return of 8.0%) outperforms MA20 which confirms the hypothesis that old tried and tested technical analysis trading rules do not perform as well as they used to (Irwin & Park, 2009; Olson, 2004). With this argument, we rule out the use of the technical rules used by Lukac et al., (1988), Brock et al., (1992), and Bessembinder and Chan (1995). BBZ which underperforms in the first period −0.5%), performs the best (52.9%) in the evaluation period. This shows that the market nature has changed to be suitable for delayed confirmed entry. Opt50 MA is consistent in its performance and can be considered for the use of future further benchmarking. The performance of AMA′ (Chan Phooi M'ng, 2018) dropped to 11.6%, reducing the average annual return for the entire period 27.4%. N-CAMA's performance continues to improve as it adjusts to the current market conditions, and its average annual return is consistent and is the highest at 36.3% per annum.

Table 7.1 Results of tested trading models for the evaluation period (2015–2017)

	Buy and hold (%)	*MA20* (%)	*MAC3,21* (%)	*MA20,0,1%* (%)	*BBZ* (%)	*Opt50MA* (%)	*AMA'* (%)	*N-CAMA'* (%)
2015	−20.1	90.1	60.1	89.3	69.6	72.5	87.5	58.0
2016	52.1	−40.6	13.2	−41.8	5.3	−12.8	−55.5	51.8
2017	15.1	−17.3	−5.6	−12.7	−24.1	−23.5	−31.8	−27.3
Sum of yearly returns	46.99	32.24	67.66	34.77	50.90	36.18	0.17	82.54
Average return per year	15.66	10.75	22.55	11.59	16.97	12.06	0.06	27.51
Cumulative return after transaction costs	23.6	99.4	146.7	126.1	158.7	90.5	34.9	144.8
Average cumulative return per year	7.9	33.1	48.9	42.0	52.9	30.2	11.6	48.3

Source Author's creation based on tests

Table 7.2 Results of tested trading models for the in-sample period (2000–2014), the evaluation period (2015–2017) and the combined period (2000–2017)

Trading models	*In sample 2000–2014 (%)*	*Out of sample 2015–2017 (%)*	*In sample and out of sample 2000–2017 (%)*
Buy and hold	8.5	7.9	8.4
MA20	3.1	33.1	7.8
MAC (3,21)	1.6	48.9	9.0
MA (20,0,1%)	4.5	42.0	6.1
BBZ	−0.5	52.9	2.1
Opt50 MA	24.2	30.2	25.2
AMA'	32.1	11.6	27.4
N-CAMA′	33.3	48.3	36.3

Source Author's creation based on tests

N-CAMA′, the best performing model so far, can be considered for further future use by analyzing its characteristics for consistent performance.

In the evaluation period, 2015–2017, as shown in Table 7.3, the average return per year is $11 compared to $10, the number of profitable trades is two times the unprofitable ones, the average gain of $0.85 to average of −1.19 is similar to the previous period. The maximum consecutive loss of $5.58 in this short period is not reflective of the loss true nature which is $38.10 in the long term.

In an institutional proprietary trading desk, trade evaluation is done jointly by the chief dealer and the trading system designer. They can run optimization tests for more fitting parameters and can also eyeball the spreadsheets of the trade evaluation journal.

Trade evaluations are done to trace a common pattern in the losing trades and to check if there is a way to get earlier confirmation for the winning trades. Slight adjustments that quicken or lessen the sensitivity of the mechanical trading systems may be made. The objective is the same, to make the least losses with maximum profits.

While periodic evaluation is conducted for audit purpose, evaluation at the end and beginning of trends would be ideal. However, it is difficult, if not impossible, to guesstimate whether the market is at the middle point of the range or trend. Thus, it is recommended that an ad hoc evaluation and

Table 7.3 Analysis of trading models' results for the evaluation period (2015–2017)

	MA20	*MA(3,21)*	*MA(20,1%)*	*BBZ*	*OptMA*	*AMA'*	*N-CAMA'*
Net cumulative profit after transaction costs (per year)	7.91	11.68	10.03	12.63	7.20	2.78	11.52
Number of profitable trades to unprofitable trades	27:72	19:40	11:32	13:32	12:55	20:75	236:141
Average profit to average loss	4.15:−1.23	5.25:−1.62	7.13:−1.32	5.31:−0.97	7.83:−1.32	5.11:−1.25	0.85:−1.19
Maximum consecutive losses	−13.33	−15.78	−16.59	−9.14	−28.73	−21.36	−5.58
	7	9	8	10	19	14	1

Source Author's creation based on tests

optimization can be conducted between the periodic evaluations. Compare the ad hoc evaluation against the periodic evaluation and adjust the parameters, if necessary, accordingly.

You can do paper trading; that is trading on live data without the use of actual capital; you may consider the evaluation period as the paper trading period or you may want to begin the paper trading after the evaluation period. Some institutions would start with the minimum capital to put pilot trading with the model and increase the size of the capital after they are confident of the efficacy to the trading model to the ever-changing markets. A paper trading result of 2018 is included in Appendix.

Capital and Risk Management

Trading strategy begins with clever capital management. Capital management is an important component of trading game because it ultimately determines if the new trader has sufficient capital to last to capture a big trend and succeed as a seasoned trader.

The amount of capital required should be computable from the start of trading based on the chosen trading model and the properties of the data series of the market that the trader wants to trade in. A common way to compute capital requirement is based on the maximum consecutive losses that we had derived earlier. The underlying concept is simply that the minimum of capital required would be maximum consecutive losses that the backtest on the trading model shows. The reason for having enough capital to sustain a series of small losses is to capture, the big gain, the "big one" when the trend finally comes.

The successful trading career must begin enough capital to provide for unfortunate periods of maximum consecutive losses. The previous maximum consecutive losses can be used to serve as a guide to future losses. We only hope that future consecutive losses will not exceed the previous known maximum consecutive losses. We should be prepared for the worst-case scenario each time we enter the market, so that we do not give up before the big trend. The big trend usually comes after a period of frustrating small losses.

The maximum consecutive losses which is one of the most important statistics in any trading model show that N-CAMA′ experienced the highest maximum consecutive losses of $38.10 for 16 consecutive trades from 23 December 2008 to 5 March 2009. This loss experience is not only psychologically damaging for the trader, but it is a set back for his equity and trading track record. The maximum consecutive drawdown is considered very high compared to the average gain of $7.94 per year and against margin requirement of USD2700. (A loss of USD38,100 would result in margin call to the trader to top up his maintenance margin at least 14 times.) In this example, the $38.10 consecutive losses came after a gain of $42 for the year 2008. Thus, the trader is able to take the losses financially and psychologically. A new trader who starts with this kind of consecutive losses would have had repeated margin calls. This shows that trading requires a lot of patience and persistence. N-CAMA′ is found to be not as attractive as it first appears to be, and further optimization and tuning especially in cutting loss are required during and after the evaluation period. For the next period, a possible stop loss may be inputted into the trading system.

For example, the maximum number of consecutive losses for N-CAMA′ for the in-sample period of 2000–2014 is 16 from 23 December 2008 to 5 March 2009, totaling 38.1 or $38,100 per contract. Psychologically, this will affect the emotional trader badly, but the professional trader will make it to the next series of gains recovering most of the losses from 24 August 2009 to 2 December 2009 totaling 33.1 or $33,100 per contract. If the apprentice trader can make it to these gains, he or she can set to be a trader for life. Therefore, in this case, enough capital per contract is the sum of the initial margin of $2700 and the maximum consecutive losses of $38,100, totaling $40,800.

The equity curve of the amount of capital in the account can be plotted (Fig. 7.1).

Note the accumulated profit/equity is growing steadily through the years and experienced sharp decline from end of August 2008 to beginning of September, beginning of January 2011 to end of June 2011.

Trading to a professional trader is all about loss management. There is no need to manage the gains. Once the losses are professionally managed, net gain will accumulate automatically.

Money management is in fact risk management with adequate capital. The important thing to remember about trading is that it is not luck when you win or lose: It is risk management and the disciplined act of cutting losses.

Once sufficient capital is prepared to handle the maximum consecutive losses before the big break comes, all the trader has to do is to concentrate on cutting losses for trading is a series of losses. The losses are not painful if the trading is conducted with discipline. An automated stop-loss order is the most disciplined and easiest way to exit the market. Professional loss cutting

Fig. 7.1 Accumulated equity using N-CAMA′ simulations from 2000 to 2018 (*Source* Author's creation based on accumulated equity using N-CAMA′ simulations from 2000 to 2018)

is done early. Lateness in cutting loss is indiscipline. Only after the new trader learnt to cut loss early, will he be qualified to become a professional trader. The disciplined act of cutting losses early is the qualifying mark of becoming a professional trader because in big trend movements, the profit amounts will exceed the small losses made in sideway markets. Trading is all about cutting losses early, so the losses are small. When the big trend profit comes, it should exceed the total amount of the small losses. Then the trader's net trading position and experience are positive.

The easiest and most professional way to execute stop loss is to place stop order at the point of entry, at the initiation of a new position. In this way, the amount of maximum loss is known at the point of entry.

From the in-sample and evaluation periods, if a stop loss of $6 had been used for N-CAMA′, the profits would have been 150 for in-sample period and 447 for evaluation period.

Conclusion: Cutting Loss Is the Key to Survival in the Trading Game

Risk management in trading is synonymous with the disciplined action of cutting losses early. Cutting losses is the first and the hardest lesson that professional traders learn and master. This is because losses should always be controlled.

Losing is part of the game. The people who do not want to lose small will almost certainly ultimately lose big. If they do not cut their losses early and the market never reverses to let them out at profit or at cost, this will ultimately result in huge losses for them.

Risk management is how to keep the losses small and let the gains run. Loss management is how to stop loss early and carry on with the trading plan. For speculative trading, there is no riskless gain; therefore, make sure your risk of loss is small, for your gain will automatically accumulate to be big, when there is a trend.

Putting your good-till-cancel (GTC) stop-loss order at the point of entry is the most disciplined and easiest way of cutting your loss. Only if the market moves in the direction of your trade should you follow with a trailing stop.

The steps to loss management are:

- Putting an automatic GTC stop loss at order at point of entry;
- Adjusting the trailing stops at each new level.

Risk management is all about cutting loss. Expect to lose and predict the amount of loss. Your trading plan should factor this in. Therefore, you should expect that loss and control it by using an automatic GTC stop-loss order. Traders must place their automatic GTC stop-loss orders at the point of entry. Their stop loss may be at such significant levels as the previous high/low or resistance/support. Some of the professional trading models use stop-loss levels that are functions of the previous day's range.

In this way, traders can calculate their losses, which must be controlled and kept low. At the point of entry, professional traders are able to calculate the maximum losses if markets go against their trading signals. There is no such thing as unexpected losses as reported in the press.

Whether the trader is long (or short) a position, the potential loss is limited to your stop-loss level. As the price rises and the long profit continues to grow, the sell stop loss can be revised up. For a short position, the buy stop loss will protect the position against further price rises. Similarly, if the price declines, the short position will profit with trailing buy stop loss that is repeatedly revised downwards.

If the stop placed, is not triggered, then the market is moving in the direction of the position. The stop may be revised in the market's direction; which is why this is called a trailing stop. Though this may be a boring mechanical way to trade but it is the most stress-free way known for repeatedly healthy profit performance.

Note that trading is a game of probability. To win, the odds must be stacked in the trader's favor. With a good trading system, the odds have been shown to be in the trader's favor. In order to calculate and control these odds, a linear trading program must be established. Linear trading means trading the same number of contracts.

Much discipline is required not to overtrade and to trade according to the plan. There is a tendency to increase the number of trading positions when the market is moving in the trader's favor. This is called pyramiding. With pyramiding, the odds can no longer be controlled. If pyramiding works against the trader's favor, it will be doubly hard to make back the profits that have been lost. In backtesting, these extra losses have not been taken into account.

In the same way, that you have an automated stop loss, the entry must be automated to the trading system that you have chosen. The entry and exit the market immediately and mechanically at the signals to do so. The technique for executing orders is to sell to the bidder or buy from the seller at the best available market price. This is to prevent missing the price because when the market trends, prices tend to run away. Some novice traders have tried to place limit orders to buy lower than the market price or sell higher than the market price only to find that the market never retraces to give them a chance to enter their positions, and prices have run away in the direction of their signals. The advice here is to forget the few points that can be gained from placing limit orders that are better than the market price. Trade at market prices because when trend signals come, the chances are high that prices will continue trending further away in the direction of the signals.

More important than placing market orders is placing a GTC stop-loss order at the point of entry. This is to prevent overloss. It is human nature to avoid losses. An automated GTC stop order at the point of entry eliminates the pain of cutting your loss at the pre-determined cut loss level. This is the professional thing to do because the expected loss can be imputed into the calculation of the risk to reward ratio. This is an important part of the trading plan.

The first cut may be painful but the last cut kills. Psychological counseling may be required in dealing with the loss the trader him or herself cuts but if the trading house ever has to cut the loss for a trader then he or she is beyond financial repair. Therefore, the first and most important lesson in trading is how to cut a loss early. Not until the new trader can learn how to take small losses and carry on trading, is he or she truly qualified as a professional trader.

To do so is to follow the cut loss trading plan, which is to place the stop-loss order at the point of entry. It is my observation that people rarely know how to cut losses themselves, so it is best when the trading system automatically does it for them. This is done by keying in a GTC stop-loss order at the onset of a new trading position.

Review

- In accordance with Random Walk hypothesis (Fama, 1965), Buy and Hold produces the highest return in 2016 and 2017; however, evaluation of the performance of the N-CAMA′ shows that it outperforms Buy and Hold in sum of yearly returns (82 vs 47%), average return per year (27 vs 15%), cumulative return after transaction costs (144 vs 23%), and average cumulative return per year (448.3 vs 7.9%).
- N-CAMA′ also outperforms its peers by the sum of returns with average return of 27.51% per annum for the 3 years in evaluation. However, upon closer analysis, in these 3 years, according to cumulative return after transaction costs, MA (3,21,0%) and BBZ outperform N-CAMA′ with average cumulative return of 48.9% and 52.9% per year against N-CAMA's average of 48.3%. This shows that the market is dynamic in nature, and its natural characteristics keep evolving such that different trading models cater better to different market periods.
- Comparing the market in the two periods (2000–2014) and (2015–2017) shows that the average cumulative return is about 8%, while N-CAMA′ gives an average cumulative return of 36% for the whole period (33% for 2000–2014 period and 48% for 2015–2017 period).
- Different trading models work better in different periods. MA20 performs badly with average cumulative return of 3.1% in the in-sample period while doing better with 33.1% average annual return in the evaluation period. In either period, the Buy and Hold (average return of 8.0%), outperforms MA20 which confirms the hypothesis that old

tried and tested technical analysis trading rules do not perform as well as they used to (Irwin & Park, 2009; Olson, 2004). BBZ which underperforms in the first period (−0.5%), performs the best (52.9%) in the evaluation period. This shows that the market nature has changed to be suitable for delayed confirmed entry. Opt50 MA is consistent in its performance and can be considered for the use of future further benchmarking. AMA's performance dropped to 11.6%, reducing the average annual return for the entire period 27.4%.

- N-CAMA's performance continues to improve as it adjusts to the current market conditions and its average annual return is consistent and is the highest at 36.3% per annum.
- N-CAMA′, the best performing model so far can be considered for further future use by analyzing its characteristics for consistent performance.
- In the evaluation period, 2015–2017, the average return per year is $11 compared to $10, the number of profitable trades is two times the unprofitable ones, and the average gain of $0.85 to average of −1.19 is similar to the previous period. The maximum consecutive loss of $5.58 in this short period is not reflective of the loss true nature which is $38.10 in the long term.
- For example, the maximum number of consecutive losses for N-CAMA′ for the in-sample period of 2000–2014 is 16 from 23 December 2008 to 5 March 2009, totaling 38.1 or $38,100 per contract. Psychologically, this will affect the emotional trader badly, but the professional trader will make it to the next series of gains recovering most of the losses from 24 August 2009 to 2 December 2009 totaling 33.1 or $33,100 per contract. If the apprentice trader can make it to these gains, he or she can set to be a trader for life. Therefore, in this case, enough capital per contract is the sum of the initial margin of $2700 and the maximum consecutive losses of $38,100, totaling $40,800.
- Note the accumulated profit/equity is growing steadily through the years and experienced sharp decline from end of August 2008 to beginning of September, beginning of January 2011 to end of June 2011.
- Trading to a professional trader is all about loss management. There is no need to manage the gains. Once the losses are professionally managed, net gain will accumulate automatically.

- Money management is in fact risk management with adequate capital. The important thing to remember about trading is that it is not luck when you win or lose: It is risk management and the disciplined act of cutting losses.
- The easiest and most professional way to execute stop loss is to place stop order at the point of entry, at the initiation of a new position. In this way, the amount of maximum loss is known at the point of entry.
- From the in-sample and evaluation periods, if a stop loss of $6 had been used for N-CAMA′, the profits would have been 150 for in-sample period and 447 for evaluation period.

Appendix

See Tables 7.4 and 7.5.

Table 7.4 Results of tested trading models for the in-sample period (2000–2014), the evaluation period (2015–2017) and the combined period (2000–2017)

	Buy and hold (%)	*MA20 (%)*	*MAC3,21 (%)*	*MA20,0,1% (%)*	*BBZ (%)*	*Opt50MA (%)*	*AMA′ (%)*	*N-CAMA′ (%)*
2000	7.21	−16.42	−0.10	−9.49	1.86	−38.63	−0.40	−8.15
2001	−23.54	−0.91	16.83	−2.03	7.33	−6.23	−11.08	−15.40
2002	37.66	17.94	28.53	9.70	−6.66	−31.03	−5.72	−23.68
2003	5.89	18.51	14.78	1.64	−1.72	18.91	−3.37	43.18
2004	37.66	−9.43	−3.30	−12.10	−18.90	−11.23	28.32	55.32
2005	42.03	32.60	4.67	−0.92	−19.46	6.59	22.77	4.13
2006	−2.53	−13.95	−11.90	−13.70	−2.14	0.39	−25.35	−0.38
2007	65.78	20.01	19.63	10.98	13.90	−9.89	22.52	49.51
2008	−46.77	42.08	−19.06	54.22	44.38	39.43	114.40	39.82
2009	46.28	−79.36	58.57	−52.14	−17.14	85.37	−48.07	−37.34
2010	9.95	−17.41	−12.83	−8.88	−15.19	−8.53	0.46	−2.43
2011	7.24	2.35	−16.63	−3.88	−19.47	24.83	21.16	24.59
2012	−8.98	7.40	−11.18	6.40	−4.43	13.87	6.93	25.24
2013	4.79	−12.03	−5.91	−10.83	−0.81	−2.08	2.31	−5.02
2014	−42.06	4.13	14.16	8.62	3.37	−6.09	3.11	2.30
2015	−20.14	90.14	60.11	89.28	69.64	72.47	87.51	58.04
2016	52.07	−40.62	13.15	−41.85	5.33	−12.77	−55.53	51.81
2017	15.06	−17.27	−5.61	−12.67	−24.07	−23.51	−31.81	−27.31
Sum of yearly returns	187.60	27.75	143.91	12.36	15.83	111.85	71.52	234.24
Average return per year	10.42	1.54	7.99	0.69	0.88	6.21	3.97	13.01
Cumulative return after transaction costs	153	140	162	111	38	454	493	654
Average cumulative return per year	8	8	9	6	2	25	27	36
2018	−26.81	−9.64	−16.29	24.41	17.24	−37.58	1.42	−3.01

Source Author's creation based on tests

Table 7.5 Results of tested trading models for the out-of-sample period (2000–2014)

	Buy and hold (%)	*MA20 (%)*	*MAC3,21 (%)*	*MA20,0,1% (%)*	*BBZ (%)*	*Opt50MA (%)*	*AMA′ (%)*	*N-CAMA′ (%)*
2018	−26.81	−9.64	−16.29	24.41	17.24	−37.58	1.42	−3.01

Source Author's creation based on tests

References

Bessembinder, H., & Chan, K. (1995, July). The profitability of technical trading rules in Asian stock markets. *Pacific-Basin Finance Journal, 3,* 257–284.

Brock, W., Lakonishok, J., & LeBaron, B. (1992, December). Simple technical trading rules and the stochastic properties of stock returns. *Journal of Finance, 47,* 1731–1764.

Chan, J. (2005, March/April). Using time series volatilities to trade trends: Trading technique—BBZ. *Australian Technical Analysts Association Journal,* 31–38.

Chan, J. (2006, March). Trading trends with the Bollinger Bands Z-Test. *Technical Analysis of Stocks & Commodities,* 46–52.

Chan, J. (2011). *Financial Times guide to technical analysis: How to trade like a professional.* London, UK: Financial Times Prentice-Hall.

Chan Phooi M'ng, J. (2018). Dynamically Adjustable Moving Average (AMA′) technical analysis indicator to forecast Asian Tigers' futures markets. *Physica A: Statistical Mechanics and Its Applications, 509,* 336–345.

Fama, E. (1965). Random walks in stock market prices. *Financial Analyst Journal, 16,* 1–16.

Irwin, S., & Park, C. (2009). A reality check on technical trading rule profits in the U.S. futures markets. *Journal of Futures Markets, 30,* 633–659.

Lukac, L., Brorsen, B., & Irwin, S. (1988). Similarity of computer guided technical trading systems. *Journal of Futures Markets, 8*(1–13), 64.

Olson, D. (2004). Have trading rule profits in the currency markets declined over time? *Journal of Banking & Finance, 28,* 85–105.

CHAPTER 8

Conclusion: End of Course and Beginning of Trading

Abstract The conclusion is never to trade without a statistically proven trading model. This last section lists out the checklist for the trader to complete the final check before he begins trading successfully. He drafts his own trading plan including many markets. To find the best trading instrument, specific research data analysis on times series and tests on the most profitable ones are done. The most suitable technical indicator, like adjustable moving average, is selected, further innovated and tested to make it work for him. He writes his own formulae into his own trading program, including the stop loss for risk management. He manages his capital well. Auditing and periodic checks on the trading journal keep the trading system updated. Completing the checklist, he starts trading.

Keywords Trading plan · Trading checklist · Statistically proven trading model · Stress test

Introduction

The primary objective of this book is to get you started trading professionally with an expectation of a net positive return. The chapters were laid out accordingly in this book to meet this overall purpose. The objective of the first part is to equip the apprentice trader with the knowledge and the tools

J. Chan, *Automation of Trading Machine for Traders*,
https://doi.org/10.1007/978-981-13-9945-9_8

of technical analysis, as the world knows it. The second part aims to discuss the research underlying the markets and technical concepts to select appropriate technical indicators and innovate them to suit the markets you want to trade in. The ultimate objective is for you to be a professional trader who makes profit in the long run.

This book is akin to a good trading plan laid out before the aspiring trader. A good trading plan is the most important component of the trader's set up as it is a map of successful trading strategies. It contains the trading rules that put the probability of winning in the long run in the trader's favor; for having a trading plan is to have a disciplined entry and exit without emotional constraint. Trading is fun and exciting, but it does not fulfill the emotional or psychological need for winning, as in other games. Trading is a probability game, and there is a 50% chance of winning and a 50% chance of losing. This is why you need to have a trading plan and strategies that give you a positive statistical profit edge.

A Trading Plan is a blueprint of trading strategies that puts together all the technical knowledge that we have to put the probability of winning in our favor.

A good trading plan specifies:

- The trading strategies;
- The mathematical mechanical model to apply;
- The amount to risk for the amount of expected reward;
- The amount of capital required to start the trading business.

Summary Review of Trading Lessons

It is most unfortunate that a lot of people put together trading plans and then fail to follow them because they are overcome by their own feelings of greed and fear. With their greed, they may try to outguess the trading system they have chosen to get earlier entries and try to make more profits. When their trades against them, their fear of admitting loss held them back from cutting the losses as indicated by the trading system that they have chosen. Trading is a game of probability. To win, the odds must be stacked in your favor. In order to calculate and control these odds, a linear trading program must be established. Linear trading means trading the same number of contracts at all times.

- A trading plan is necessary because it specifies the amount to risk for the amount of reward to expect. The most important element in a trading plan is the maximum permissible loss. This permissible loss is determined by the stop-loss order placed at the initiation of the trade. The algorithm technical trading system to use is the one that makes the most profit, with the least consecutive losses and with at least equal chances of profitable trades and losing trades.
- Writing out the trading plan is a very necessary procedure and acting on the trading signals automatically may take the gambling fun of trading, but it will make you a professional trader.
- The fun is in finding the algorithm technical trading system that suits the most lucrative market that you can find and also your personality.

Trading Strategy of Trading Plan

Trading is a probability game. If we can calculate the probability and probable magnitude of winning, we can draw a detailed plan to encompass the possible outcomes of trading. If we can draw the binomial outcome tree with short losing branches and long winning branches, we can calculate the net probability of winning. This translates as the 50:50 rule that says if there are equal chances of winning and losing trades, the trading edge must lie in the larger magnitude of wins versus controlled losses.

To a trader, it is very important to be able to draw the binomial probabilities of outcomes and calculate beforehand the net result of this business. Without a trading plan, the trader is lost, completely on his or her own, with primitive greed and fears. The trader has nothing to aim for, nothing to guide him or her, and nothing to control losses. Most likely, he or she does not even have a mathematical mechanical model, like most amateur traders who enter the market on tips and rumors.

The trader must not reveal his or her trading plan to others, especially other traders. The trading plan must be private, especially the stop losses. This is because scalpers will try to make a living from triggering your stop losses. The trick is to place your stops where they will not be triggered unnecessarily.

The most important part of the trading plan is the money management and risk management components. Profiting from the trading plan is achieved by controlling the losses. All losses must be small. This is part of money management.

You have to start somewhere sometime and it may as well as be with the market you are most familiar with when you are prepared, mentally and financially. You start when you have a trading plan. A trading plan is one of the elements that distinguishes a successful, profitable trader to one who is not.

In conclusion, it all starts and ends with a trading plan.

The most important conclusion that we are able to draw from all that we have learnt is never to trade without a statistically proven trading model.

In this book, we have laid out the steps to build a basic professional trading model; the process involves first data analysis in order to choose the right market, tools, techniques, formulas, and software. The most important element of a trading plan and trading system is its risk management which emphasizes how to control the losses. Without a stop-loss order at the point of entry, there is no way for the trader to guesstimate his chances of winning against losing. Capital must be sufficient to cover periods of consecutive losses. Trades must be evaluated periodically to check what went right, what went wrong and how the model can be further improved. A trading system fine-tuning and improvement can be done after a large gain following a period of small consecutive losses.

If the amount of money that you risk in trading represents a minuscule fraction of your net worth, and you are not concerned about your profit, then you trade professionally without any worries.

If you are trading, you should be serious about it. Capital and time are hard earned and should be invested wisely.

Trading Checklist

This final section list out the checklist for you to do the final check before you begin to trade successfully.

Review this book carefully before you begin to take the first steps in trading.

1. Draft your own trading plan, you may include in as many markets as there are to trade. The whole universe is your test ground. However, not every market is your trade market.
2. To find the best trading ground, you have do your own research; that to do data analysis on all the time series you can find and test, innovate and stress test the most profitable ones.

3. You have to select the most suitable technical indicator for the markets that you are testing, you innovate the most suitable technical indicator, like moving average and then stress test this innovated technical indicator to make it work for you.
4. Write your own formulae into your own trading program.
5. Include in the stop loss for risk management purpose.
6. Calculate and keep excess for your capital management.
7. Keep a trading journal for audit and revision purpose.
8. Do periodic check and revise from step one.
9. Start trading.

Trading Plan

If you based your trading decision on tips, then you are another rumor monger. You will be doing what the large fund managers want you to do, buy when they sell, sell when they buy. Is that what you want? Follow their trading plan or follow your own? To make losses or money? If you do not have a trading plan, you are not ready to trade. The more specific the trading plan is, the better is your trading strategy. The trading strategy is to specify the trading system, the trading rules. Your trading system should be well tested before you put your first bet, that is, your trade on it.

Check Your Trading Plan for the Market You Wish to Trade In

Know the characteristics of the markets that you want to trade in. If capital allows, always look at a few active markets to trade. Always keep watch on a few markets for the one that can give the largest directional trade profit. To do this, you must set aside time and available funds. You need to monitor a few markets and instruments to trade in, so that you can take advantage of the most volatile directional market. By trading a range of markets, you have a better chance of catching good directional trades based on volatility.

Do Your Own Research, Data Analysis and Testing, Innovation, and Stress Testing

Different markets offer different market scenarios, and trading different markets will eventually ensure that the trading the right instruments in one of the right markets.

Research includes data analysis; gather, compile, and organize your data into in-sample period and out-of-sample period.

Analyze the data, that is, what kind of mean and standard deviation that it experiences per year and most importantly if there is any kurtosis in the data. The kurtosis will give the large returns. Take note of your observations and test them, if you can.

It is good if you can build a trading system from scratch, but if you cannot do so, use the best existing known trading system first. For the market that you are interested to trade in, do a best trading system test/simulation using Bloomberg, Metastock, and the likes, and sort in terms of profits for the in-sample data. Using that same trading system, perform the test on the out-of-sample data.

If the results are consistently among the best, then do any optimization test on the parameter (for as large a range as possible) for the in-sample period. Using that optimized parameter, test to see if the good result is reflected again in the out-of-sample period.

If the results for both periods are consistently good, then you may have find yourself a good trading system for that particular market you tested.

The next step is to see if your trading system with that optimized parameter can work just as well (the same kind of percentage return) for both in-sample and out-of-sample data for other markets that you intend to trade in, in the future.

If it does, all is well. If it does not, do optimization test on each of those markets as different markets have different characteristics. Then, if using the optimized parameter works well for both in-sample and out-of-sample data, then you have yourself a different parameter trading system for different markets.

However, sometimes, a parameter that works well for the in sample, does not work as well for out-of-sample period. It may be that market condition has changed. If that is the case, then periodically, the system needs to be optimized to suit the current market condition.

Select the Most Suitable Technical Indicator for Your Market

The most popular technical indicators may not be the best simply because they are the most common and many similar orders are placed at the same trigger places. However, having said that, the most common technical indicators are the most popular because they were effective in making profit and were profitable in the past. However, with the common use of these technical indicators like simple moving averages, these indicators are less effective in the present, faster-moving market. Therefore, a slight modification to the parameters of these common technical indicators is generally sufficient. It is up to the individual trader to modify some of these technical indicators to suit the market that he would like to trade in, like making moving average into an adaptive or adjustable moving average trading system.

Have a Risk Control Mechanism in Your Trading System

The rigid control of losses is the most critical prerequisite for long-term profit. A trading plan should include: Maximum risk per trade

By restricting your loss by specifying the maximum percentage of your total fund that you can lose per trade, you will have better chances of surviving the long-term as a profitable winner.

The risk can be restricted to the stop-loss level. Put in your stop loss good-till-cancel order immediately after you have initiated a trade. Stop loss is the only way to exit your trade. Without an automated stop-loss order, our human nature is prone to procrastinating the decision to cut loss when the level arrives.

To win the simple probability game, the number of contracts traded should be the same. This is called linear trading.

Calculate and Keep Excess for Your Capital Management

Having enough capital is a good start to successful trading. The question is how much is enough capital? The simple answer is to have enough capital to last through the bad times. It would be really unfortunate for the would-be trader to begin his trading career at the beginning of period maximum consecutive losses. However, if he had sufficient capital to last through this period of consecutive losses and make it to the next gain, he would have passed the trial of being a professional trader. Never give up on your trading system and your trading before the big gain. The big gain is there, waiting for you if you can get to it.

Keep a Trading Journal for Audit and Revision Purpose

It is best to maintain a trading journal which you can review. It is important to keep record of every trade, electronically and in book entry as in days of old. The purpose of faithfully keeping record in your trading journal is for future audit and evaluation. Carefully evaluate what went right and what went wrong. If the trader strictly follows the trading signal, even if it resulted in a loss, he would have been alright. However, what went wrong can be that the trader did not follow the trading system and if he does not, then the chances of controlling his loss are low and capital depletion is high. The purpose of the trade evaluation is to assess the actual realized return against the projected return and the actual realized losses against the permissible risk. If followed with discipline, the actual realized losses should be the stop-loss levels or the permissible risk. You have to trade every trade automatically according to your algorithm so that you can calculate the probability of your losses.

Do Periodic Check and Revise from Step One

A periodical postmortem of trade evaluation sheets should be undertaken to trace a common pattern in the losing trades and to check if there is a way to get earlier confirmation for the winning trades. Slight adjustments that quicken or lessen the sensitivity of the mechanical trading systems may be made.

On reflection, it is important after winning a big one, as I call it, to review your trading system. On hindsight you could have done better if you had changed your system like this. I never give up on my systems halfway, that is, I do not abandon my trading system in the middle of a series of losses. I do not abandon them then is because often traders give up just before the big trend comes. Therefore, I usually review my trading system after the big one.

Evaluate your trading which includes your discipline especially in cut loss situations. The trader who knows how to cut loss is the long-term trader. Use your trading journal to evaluate your trading model. Decide on a specific protective stop at the time of entry. Always get out immediately once your stop is triggered.

Lastly, Start Trading

You have read enough about others' trading and mistakes. You have done your research. You have to start when you are ready.

Conclusion: Last Words—The Market Is Always Right

The last word to the apprentice trader is do not take small profits, just follow your trading system. Use trailing stops to get out. Ride on the trend as far as it takes you. Take as much profit as the market wants to give you. Never underestimate the market, the market is always right.

Patience is important not only in waiting for the right trades but also in staying with trades that are working. The failure to adequately profit from correct trades is a key profit limiting factor.

Model trading is simple and without real-life emotions. Trading in reality is much more dangerous than paper model trading. Professional traders agree that they can define and control the dangers. The known dangers are slippage, not getting filled at the triggered price but at some price worse than the stop-loss price, and prices whipsawing.

Therefore, the results from backtesting can be different from the actual profit from live trading. This can be due to slippage, that is, we may not get the price we want because of thin market conditions, intraday whipsaws (the market may give false signals, i.e., touch the trigger price and move back to where it came from) and extra rollover transaction costs (the signal is still on, the month is expiring and we need to roll over to the next month).

Is trading futures for you? Trading futures for a living takes years of research, besides incurring many trading losses, to find a trading model that you can bet your money on. Futures are highly leveraged instrument as they use small margins as collateral. Therefore, the risk exposure and loss potential are huge as are the gains. As in finance theory, for the high amount of risk exposure, you expect high amount of rewards. Trading futures involves managing and controlling the risks and losses. Good money management entails having enough cash flow to trade a big trend after a series of small losses. If you can manage your capital and make it to grow, you have the qualifications to become a professional trader. Therefore, before you take the leap to become a professional trader, make sure you have the discipline to follow your trading system to make your capital last and grow. Of course, you must have sufficient capital as determined by your ability to withstand a series of continuous losses due to whipsaws.

Review

- Those who never want to cut a loss will be the losers when they are forced to do so when all their margins are depleted.
- They, of course, do not follow any trading plan or system because all trading plans or systems have cut loss stops at the entry point.
- Long-term winners follow trading systems and cut losses whenever the stop-loss prices are triggered. Long-term winners also never give up after a series of small losses because they believe in their chosen trading systems and they do not change them before the big gain.
- By reading this book, you have taken a shortcut through years of losses and research to become a professional trader.
- When you are trading, avoid the emotional trap of wanting to be 100% correct. In other words, trail your stop carefully. You may opt for the concept of parabolic stop. Always pay attention to market action rather than your objectives and support/resistance area.
- When your trading system tells you to enter, do so immediately. When your trading system tells you to exit, do so automatically. Never go countertrend to your trading system.
- All trading signals must be mechanically followed with strict discipline. If you pick and choose the signals that coincide with fundamental research reports generated by broking houses, they are almost always the wrong signals—ones that result in losses. The trading plan is what separates the professional trader from the amateur. A trading plan must include a risk management mechanism, I call, the early cutloss program. As long as there are cutloss orders at the point of entry of each trade, the net result of any disciplined trading can only be profit because market trends. The ones who follow the rules strictly with discipline become professional traders. The rest remain gamblers who make big profits and bigger losses because they are ruled by greed.
- Trading is the most exciting profession in the world for me and I hope it is for you too. It is a serious profession because it involves people's life savings. I know you are serious about trading because you took the time to read this book to the end. There is only one way to get start—chart your own trading. Use the tools in this book to start trading and as time goes on and changes, you will develop your own unique trading system with the concepts discussed here. Many others have done it and so can you.

- I hope that the technical analysis concepts work for you as they do for many others. You are now on a level playing ground with other professional traders. The next step is to rise above this level, to be the few who profit consistently and trade for a living.

Here, it goes again, my famous ten trading rules

1. Always do your own research; no one else can do it for you. Avoid listening to rumors and tips. If they knew, they would trade it and not let you have privy information.
2. Forget about other people's trades, concentrate on yours, in particular your stop loss.
3. Stop loss and stop are the only ways to exit the markets, let the stop loss decide your loss at the point of entry and let your trailing stop determine your profit. Trailing your stop as the market move to new level in your favor.
4. Cut your stop early but never take your profit early. It would be traders' remorse to watch the profit that would have been his if he had followed his trading system. From experience, traders' remorse is worse than an actual small loss.
5. Follow your trading system. That is what they are there for. Have no fear, your trading system is here.
6. Your trading and trading system can change as time change. Make sure you change fast enough.
7. Trade the most volatile directional market and the profits are yours.
8. Never abandon your trading system half way or you will be left with losses you cannot manage.
9. Never be too arrogant about your trading profit and never boast about your trading system. Make your profits quietly and enjoy them.
10. Have fun. Trading is fun, when you win in the long run. If you can last through the largest series of losses known to make it to the next gain, then you are in, you are a trader for life.

I am restating the same thing, maybe in different words but they are the same old advice.

You have got what it takes to be an exceptional trader—the positive statistical edge of abnormal returns. You have got a unique trading tool that is your very own, innovated specially for your market to help you make the abnormal returns you can expect. As an exceptional trader, there is no room or need for luck. Trading is a serious business but it is also fun. Have fun with your fund—let it grow and build to last. Note that I said, let it grow, not make it grow because with a proven technical trading system, the abnormal returns come automatically and naturally.

Have fun, enjoy your trading and your life.

Appendix

See Table 8.1.

Table 8.1 Results of tested trading models for the entire period (2000–2018)

	Buy and Hold (%)	*MA20 (%)*	*MAC 3,21 (%)*	*MA 20,0,1% (%)*	*BBZ (%)*	*Opt50MA (%)*	*AMA' (%)*	*N-CAMA' (%)*
2000	7.21	−16.42	−0.10	−9.49	1.86	−38.63	−0.40	−8.15
2001	−23.54	−0.91	16.83	−2.03	7.33	−6.23	−11.08	−15.40
2002	37.66	17.94	28.53	9.70	−6.66	−31.03	−5.72	−23.68
2003	5.89	18.51	14.78	1.64	−1.72	18.91	−3.37	43.18
2004	37.66	−9.43	−3.30	−12.10	−18.90	−11.23	−28.32	55.32
2005	42.03	32.60	4.67	−0.92	−19.46	6.59	22.77	4.13
2006	−2.53	−13.95	−11.90	−13.70	−2.14	0.39	−25.35	−0.38
2007	65.78	20.01	19.63	10.98	13.90	−9.89	22.52	49.51
2008	−46.77	42.08	−19.06	54.22	44.38	39.43	114.40	39.82
2009	46.28	−79.36	58.57	−52.14	−17.14	85.37	−48.07	−37.34
2010	9.95	−17.41	−12.83	−8.88	−15.19	−8.53	0.46	−2.43
2011	7.24	2.35	−16.63	−3.88	−19.47	24.83	21.16	24.59
2012	−8.98	7.40	−11.18	6.40	−4.43	13.87	6.93	25.24
2013	4.79	−12.03	−5.91	−10.83	−0.81	−2.08	2.31	−5.02
2014	−42.06	4.13	14.16	8.62	3.37	−6.09	3.11	2.30
2015	−20.14	90.14	60.11	89.28	69.64	72.47	87.51	58.04
2016	52.07	−40.62	13.15	−41.85	5.33	−12.77	−55.53	51.81
2017	15.06	−17.27	−5.61	−12.67	−24.07	−23.51	−31.81	−27.31
2018	−26.81	−9.64	−16.29	24.41	17.24	−37.58	1.42	−3.01
Sum of yearly returns	160.80	18.12	127.62	36.77	33.06	74.28	72.94	231.23
Average return per year	8.46	0.95	6.72	1.94	1.74	3.91	3.84	12.17
Cumulative return after transaction costs	125	122	128	260	175	358	521	647.17
Average cumulative return per year	6.60	6.44	6.75	13.69	9.20	18.87	27.40	34.06

Source Author's creation based on tests

Glossary

Analysis

Fundamental Analysis—The study of macroeconomic industry, and asset information to estimate intrinsic value to determine if an asset is overvalued or undervalued and to forecast future price.
Technical Analysis—The study of price movements using historical prices volume, and open interest to identify time patterns and trend for the purpose of finding trading opportunities. Technical analysis includes a variety of techniques such as chart analysis, pattern recognition, and algorithm technical trading systems.

Chart Analysis

Chart—A graphical record of prices and volume taken at regular intervals.
Close/Closing Price—The last traded price for the period.
High—The highest price traded for the period.
Low—The lowest price traded for the period.
Open/Opening Price—The first traded price for the period.
Open Interest—The number of futures contracts that had been opened and had not been closed. The amount of futures contracts that are still open and in existence.
Volume—The number of contracts/shares traded for the period.

J. Chan, *Automation of Trading Machine for Traders*,
https://doi.org/10.1007/978-981-13-9945-9

Technical Indicators

Adjustable Moving Average Prime (AMA′)—A technical trading system devised in this study that uses Efficacy Ratio (a derivative of Efficient Ratio) to vary the length of the moving averages according to prevailing market conditions, avoiding some whipsaws in ranging markets and entering positions early in trend markets.
Bands—Lines constructed around a moving average that define relative high and low.
B Band Z-Test-Statistics (BBZ)—A technical trading system that uses as a default one standard deviation around a default 21-day moving average (to give long signal above the one standard deviation band and to give short signal below the one standard deviation band).
Moving Average (MA)—The measure of the average price over the previous x periods that is recomputed each succeeding period using the most recent data.
Moving Averages Crossover (MAC)—A technical indicator that uses the short-term moving crossing over the long-term moving average to indicate a buy signal when the short-term moving average crosses over the long-term moving average from below to above and a sell signal when the short-term moving average crosses over the long-term moving average from above to below.
Optimized Moving Average (OptMA)—A simple moving average which the length parameter is chosen after a series of simulations on hindsight because it generates the most profit in the past. It is used as a benchmark of what the best result that could have been had the most ideal length moving average parameter been chosen.
Momentum—A leading indicator that show the rate of change. The simplest momentum calculation is the difference between today's close and the close *n* days ago as a percentage of the close n days ago. Neural network enhanced Close and Adjustable Moving Average Prime (N-CAMA′)—A technical trading system devised in this study that uses non linear autoregressive exogenous inputs to vary weights between the Close and AMA′.

Trading Range Terms

Trading Range—A price range between resistance at the top and support at the bottom in which trading had been confined for an extended period. Generally, it is sideways in character.
Trading Range System—A trading system that tries to sell at the resistance and to buy at the support on the assumption that market will pullback at the resistance and support.
Resistance—An area where price advances halt and reverse below. It is believed that investors who bought at those higher prices will become sellers when those prices are reached again thus halting an advance.
Support—An area where price declines halt and reverse above. Support is often associated with perceived value.

Trading Trend Terms

Algorithm Trading System—A trading system with a preset of trading rules to mathematically compute according to an algorithm (suitable to the prevailing market conditions) mechanically generated signals (long, short or out-of-market) on when to enter and when to exit, and executes the trades automatically. Algorithmic trading is the computer program that executes trades according to an algorithm that is suitable to the prevailing market conditions. The algorithm in the program is derived after intensive backtesting and optimization. Algorithm trading program is popularly employed by professional model trading desks of large financial institutions.
Trend Trading System—A trading system with a set of trading rules that defines when to initiate a position early to capture the prevailing trend using a mechanically generated signal on the assumption that the trend will continue. Moving average and standard deviation are technical indicators used in trend trading system.
Downtrend—A state in which prices are steadily declining.
Uptrend—A state in which prices are steadily increasing.

Tests

Backtest—The process of testing using historical data.
Optimization—The process of finding the best performing parameter for a trading system.
Parameter—A value assigned to a trading system to vary/optimize the timing of the signal.

Theories

Dow Theory—An observation (initially by Charles Dow) that states that:

1. The averages (industrial and transportation) must confirm each other.
2. The averages discount everything.
3. The market has three movements.
4. The major trends have three phases.
5. Volume must confirm trend.
6. A trend continues until signal reverses.

Fractal Geometry—An observation (initially by Benoit Mandelbrot) that states that there are repeating patterns in nature including time series.
Random-Walk Theory—An observation (initially by Eugene Fama) that states that the past history of the series can not be used to predict the future in any meaningful way and that the future path of the price of a security is no more predictable than the path of a series of cumulated random numbers (Fama 1965).

Trading Terms

Long—The state of owning a security.
Short—The state of being short a security. The act of selling before buying.
Rollover—The closing of the front-month position and the opening of the next-month position.
Slippage Cost—The cost of the difference between the theoretical execution price and the actual price executed due to poor fill.

Volatility—The tendency for prices to vary. Standard deviation and variance are measures of volatility.
Whipsaw—A period of wrong signals.

Bibliography

Andrada-Felix, J., & Fernandex-Rodriguez, F. (2008). Improving moving average trading rules with boosting and statistical learning methods. *Journal of Forecasting, 27*, 433–449.

Atsalakis, G. S., & Valavanis, K. P. (2009). Surveying stock market forecasting techniques—Part II: Soft computing methods. *Expert Systems with Applications, 36*(3), 5932–5941.

Azizan, N. A., Mohamed, I., & Chan Phooi M'ng, J. (2011a). Profitability of technical analysis indicators: A study of an adjustable technical indicator, ABZ', on the Malaysian futures markets. *The Business Review, 7*(2), 286–290.

Azizan, N. A., Mohamed, I., & Chan Phooi M'ng, J. (2011b). A profitability study on the Malaysian futures markets using a new adjustable technical analysis indicator, ABZ. *African Journal of Business Management, 5*, 5984–5993.

Bahrammirzaee, A. (2010). A comparative survey of artificial intelligence applications in finance: Artificial neural networks, expert system and hybrid intelligent systems. *Neural Computing and Applications, 19*(8), 1165–1195.

Balsara, N., Carlson, K., & Rao, N. (1996). Unsystematic futures profits with technical trading rules: A case for flexibility. *Journal of Financial and Strategic. Decisions, 9*, 57–66.

Bessembinder, H., & Chan, K. (1995, July). The profitability of technical trading rules in Asian stock markets. *Pacific-Basin Finance Journal, 3*, 257–284.

Bessembinder, H., & Chan, K. (1998). Market efficiency and the returns to technical analysis. *Financial Management, 27*(2), 5–17.

Bollinger, J. (2002). *Bollinger on Bollinger*. New York: McGraw-Hill.

J. Chan, *Automation of Trading Machine for Traders*,
https://doi.org/10.1007/978-981-13-9945-9

Brock, W., Lakonishok, J., & LeBaron, B. (1992, December). Simple technical trading rules and the stochastic properties of stock returns. *Journal of Finance, 47*(5), 1731–1764.

Cevik, S., & Sedik, T. (2011). *A barrel of oil or a bottle of wine: How do global growth dynamics affect commodity prices?* (Working Paper 11/01). Washington, DC: International Monetary Fund.

Chan, J. (2005, March/April). Using time series volatilities to trade trends: Trading technique—BBZ. *Australian Technical Analysts Association Journal*, 31–38.

Chan, J. (2006, March). Trading trends with the Bollinger bands Z-Test. *Technical Analysis of Stocks & Commodities, 24*(3), 46–52.

Chan, J. (2011). *Financial Times guide to technical analysis: How to trade like a professional.* London, UK: Financial Times Prentice-Hall.

Chan Phooi M'ng, J. (2018). Dynamically adjustable moving average (AMA') technical analysis indicator to forecast Asian Tigers' futures markets. *Physica A: Statistical Mechanics and Its Applications, 509*, 336–345.

Chan Phooi M'ng, J., & Mehralizadeh, M. (2016). Forecasting East Asian indices futures via a novel hybrid of wavelet-PCA denoising and artificial neural network models. *PLOS One, 11*(6), e0156338.

Edwards, R. D., & Magee, J. (2008). *Technical analysis of stock trends* (9th ed.). Chicago, IL: John Magee Inc.

Fama, E. (1965). Random walks in stock market prices. *Financial Analyst Journal, 16*, 1–16.

Fernández-Pérez, A., Fernández-Rodríguez, F., & Sosvilla-Rivero, S. (2012). Detecting trends in the foreign exchange markets. *Applied Economics Letters, 19*(5), 493–503.

Fernandez-Rodnguez, F., Gonzalez-Martel, C., & Sosvilla-Rivero, S. (2000). On the profitability of technical trading rules based on artificial neural networks: Evidence from the Madrid stock market. *Economic Letters, 69*(1), 89–94.

Gandolfi, G., Rossolini, M., Sabatini, A., & Caselli, S. (2008). Dynamic MACD standard deviation embedded in MACD indicator for accurate adjustment to financial market dynamics. *International Federation of Technical Analysts Journal*, 16–23.

Gencay, R., & Stengos, T. (1998). Moving average rules, volume and the predictability of security returns with feedforward networks. *Journal of Forecasting, 17*, 401–414.

Graham, B., & Dodd, D. (1934). *Security analysis* (1st ed.). New York: Whittlesey House.

Hamilton, W. (1922). *The stock market barometer.* New York: Nabu Press.

Irwin, S., & Park, C. (2009). A reality check on technical trading rule profits in the U.S. futures markets. *Journal of Futures Markets, 30*, 633–659.

Kaastra, I., & Boyd, M. (1996). Designing a neural network for forecasting financial and economic time series. *Neurocomputing, 10*(3), 215–236.

Kwon, K. Y., & Kish, R. (2002). A comparative study of technical trading strategies and return predictability: An extension of Brock, Lakonishok, and LeBaron (1992) using NYSE and NASDAQ indices. *Quarterly Review of Economics and Finance, 42*, 611–631.

Lane, G. (1982). Lane's stochastic. *Traders' Magazine*.

Lee, C., Gleason, K., & Mathur, I. (2001). Trading rule profits in Latin American currency spot rates. *International Review of Financial Analysis, 10*(2), 135–159.

Lo, A., Mamaysky, H., & Wang, J. (2000). Foundations of technical analysis: Computational algorithms, statistical inference and empirical implementation. *Journal of Finance, 55*(4), 1705–1765.

Lukac, L., Brorsen, B., & Irwin, S. (1988). Similarity of computer guided technical trading systems. *Journal of Futures Markets, 8*(1–13), 64.

Lukac, L., Brorsen, B., & Irwin, S. (1990). *A comparison of twelve technical trading systems*. Greenville, SC: Traders Press Inc.

Malkiel, G. (1973). *A random walk down wall street* (11th ed.). New York: W. W. Norton.

Mandelbrot, B. (1967). The variation of the prices of cotton, wheat and railroad stocks and of some financial rates. *The Journal of Business, 40*, 393–413.

Mandelbrot, B., & Hudson, R. (2004). *The (mis)behaviour of markets: A fractal view of risk, ruin and reward*. London: Profile Books Ltd.

Menkhoff, L., & Taylor, M. P. (2006). *The obstinate passion of foreign exchange professionals: Technical analysis* (Warwick Economics Research Paper 872), 870–912.

Murphy, J. (1999). *Technical analysis of the financial markets*. New York: Wiley.

Nelson, S. (1903). *The ABC of stock speculation*. New York: S.A. Nelson.

Olson, D. (2004). Have trading rule profits in the currency markets declined over time? *Journal of Banking & Finance, 28*, 85–105.

Podobnik, B., & Stanley, H. (2008). Detrended cross-correlation analysis: A new method for analysing two nonstationary time series. *Physical Review Letters, 100*(8), 084102.

Rhea, R. (1932). *The Dow theory*. New York: Fraser Publishing Co.

Siegelmann, H. T., Horne, B. G., & Giles, C. L. (1997). Computational capabilities of recurrent NARX neural networks. *IEEE Transactions on Systems, Man, and Cybernetics, Part B: Cybernetics, 27*(2), 208–215.

Stanley, E., Plerou, X., & Xavier, G. (2008). A statistical physics view of financial fluctuations: Evidence for scaling and universality. *Physica A: Statistical Mechanics and its Applications, 387*(15), 3967–3981.

Taylor, M., & Allen, H. (1992). The use of technical analysis in the foreign exchange market. *Journal of International Money and Finance, 11*(3), 304–314.

Wilder, W. (1978). *New concepts in technical trading systems*. New York: Trend Research.

Yao, J., Chew, L. T., & Poh, H.-L. (1999). Neural networks for technical analysis: A study on KLCI. *International Journal of Theoretical and Applied Finance, 2*(2), 221–241.

Index

J. Chan, *Automation of Trading Machine for Traders*,
https://doi.org/10.1007/978-981-13-9945-9

CPSIA information can be obtained
at www.ICGtesting.com
Printed in the USA
LVHW070325071219
639747LV00009B/83/P

9 789811 399442